THE CONTEMPLATIVE HEART

THE CONTEMPLATIVE HEART

JAMES FINLEY

SORIN BOOKS   Notre Dame, Indiana

TO MAUREEN

In simply being who she is and in the love we share I find daily sources of inspiration and encouragement concerning the path of self-transformation this book explores.

International Standard Book Number 1-893732-10-X
Library of Congress Catalog Card Number: 99-066883
Cover design by Angela Moody
Interior text design by Brian C. Conley
Printed and bound in the United States of America.

CONTENTS

Acknowledgments

I wish to express my gratitude to the following people for the contributions they made to the writing of this book.

My wife, Maureen Fox, has been an advisor and support throughout the entire process of writing this book. My friend and colleague Bob Weathers, Ph.D., met with me on a regular basis to discuss issues and concerns I had in the writing of this book. I am grateful, too, for the time he spent assisting my wife, Maureen, with the editing of the final draft. Frank Cunningham, publisher of Sorin Books, has been patient and supportive throughout the entire process of writing of this book. His gentle proddings and insightful suggestions are greatly appreciated. Also appreciated is the supportive manner in which Bob Hamma, editorial director of Sorin Books, worked with me on the manuscript.

I also wish to express my gratitude to the following people for their support and helpful comments: Sister Mary Luke Tobin, S.L., Sr. Rose Annette Liddell, S.L., Rev. Thomas Stella, C.S.C., Rev. Thomas Keating, O.C.S.O., Gustave Reininger, Michael and Antoinette Voûte Roeder, Rev. Thomas Hand, S.J., Rev. Donald B. Cozzens, Patrick Finley, Ph.D., and Robert Doud, Ph.D.

A Note to the Reader

The first chapter of this book begins with introductory information about how and why this book was written and ends with a brief overview of its basic structure. Here, however, I wish to offer a suggestion about how to read this book based on my own understanding of its nature and purpose and my experience of writing it.

Although I was born and raised in the Roman Catholic tradition of the church to which I still belong, and although these reflections contain numerous references to Christian sources, these reflections are not intended to be representative of Christian thought.

Although I have been influenced by Buddhist teachings, ever since Thomas Merton first introduced them to me at the monastery many years ago, and although references to Buddhist sources are found throughout these reflections, these reflections are not intended to be representative of Buddhist thought.

Although I am a clinical psychologist, and although these reflections contain a number of references to psychological theory and perspectives, these reflections are not intended to be representative of any school of psychological thought.

For, in fact, these writings do not have their basis in thought, at least not the kind of thought consisting of theoretical paradigms of reality, intended to define or describe in conceptual terms such notions as God, the self, the spiritual path, or psychological healing. These writings give primacy, not to conceptual thought, but to intuitions, intimations, and experiences of the spiritual path of contemplative self-transformation. These writings are not so much poetic prose as they are prose-like poetry that seeks to voice certain fundamental experiences of self-transformation. More specifically, I have written these reflections in such a way as to evoke the contemplative experience being written about. Thus, writing these reflections has been for me a contemplative practice—a way of awakening, deepening, and sustaining the contemplative experience of the present moment.

I suggest, then, that you read these reflections slowly, much as you would listen to music. Reading these reflections in this way, your heart might resonate with mine in intimate awakenings of the contemplative experience you are reading about. To the extent this occurs, my intention in publishing these reflections will be realized. For it is in this mutual resonance of our hearts with depths too deep for thoughts to grasp, too deep for words to utter, that you and I will be communicating with one another in the graced event in which one seeker passes on to another something of the heart's contagious yearnings for the inexhaustible.

PART ONE:

A CONTEMPLATIVE VISION OF LIFE

1. Seeking a More Contemplative Way of Life

These reflections on contemplative living have their origin in the five years that I lived as a monk at the cloistered Trappist monastery of the Abbey of Gethsemani in Kentucky. Five years is not very long compared to the long haul of a lifetime in the cloister, but it was long enough to have a profound and lasting impression on me. I left the monastery with a question firmly established within me: How can I live, out here "in the world," the contemplative way of life I lived in the monastery? It has been nearly thirty years since I left the monastery—about three reincarnations ago is what it feels like, relative to how much I have changed and all that has happened. But the question of contemplative living has continued to endure, undergoing its own transformations as it has continued to transform me in my ongoing response to it. It is this ongoing response that I share with you here by presenting where I have come thus far in understanding the fundamental principles of the contemplative path.

I hope and trust that these reflections are true to the spirit of Thomas Merton, Meister Eckhart, Eihei Dogen, and the other sources of contemplative wisdom quoted and referred to in these pages. Each is among the formative influences that have contributed to the vision expressed and explored in this primer of contemplative living.

As with any primer, the focus of these reflections is on the basics: What is contemplative experience? How is contemplative experience cultivated? How do we yield to the depths of divinity that contemplative experience discloses? And in so doing, how do we become the contemplative person we, deep down, really are and long to be? We can begin our exploration of such fundamental questions of contemplative living by situating them within the broader context of a particularly contemplative way of understanding the universal human experience of being a seeker.

To be a seeker is to be someone for whom a grace has engendered a riddle. By grace is meant that which is truly real and precious simply appearing prior to and beyond one's own efforts to achieve or produce it. And by riddle is meant the "I-cannot-get-to-the-bottom-of-it" nature of the grace that is granted. All the more bewildering is the way the grace rises up out of the very substance of one's life, making the riddle to be: What will become of me if I were to surrender completely to this grace? What will become of me if I do not?

There is the grace of a man and woman falling in love with one another. The love arises as a great gift that overwhelms. And from this simply arising gift is engendered the riddle of the rest of their lives as being affected to the core by all the ways they choose to respond or not to respond to the grace of love. In similar fashion, a couple discovering they are pregnant is a grace engendering the ongoing riddle of all that parenthood will ask of them. Being a devout believer in a religious tradition is a grace engendering the riddle encountered in attempting to live as one's faith calls one to live. Seeing what justice demands is a grace, engendering the riddles encountered in embracing what justice demands. Discovering one is an artist is a grace engendering the riddle encountered in setting out to become the artist one knows deep down in one's bones one is called to be. There is, too, the grace of the awe-inspiring instant of sensing the inexhaustible nature of what is most simple and commonplace in daily living, engendering the riddles encountered in learning to reverence the incomprehensible stature of simple things.

In using the term *seeker* in a manner suggested by these examples, it can be said that each of us is a seeker of sorts in that it is according to this grace-engendering-a-riddle rhythm that our lives unfold. If we stop and ask ourselves how we have come to be who we have thus far come to be, we invariably come upon our own unique life up till now as a pattern of many graces engendering many riddles. The riddles, when faced and lived through, engender in turn more graces, engendering yet further riddles, engendering yet further graces. We become wiser, more rich with life experience as we are intimately awakened and responsive to this process in which, as we pass through life, life passes through us, transforming us in unforeseeable ways.

There is, too, the grace of desiring to live a more contemplative way of life. This desire, being a grace, is always somewhat hidden and mysterious, remaining that which simply arises without our being able to give an adequate accounting as to the why and wherefore of it all. We are, however, often able to look back to see the matrix of intimate experience in which the grace first appeared. Upon such reflection this matrix often proves to be the moments of grace that engender the riddles of our life. We see how in our moments of love, birth, religious experience, justice, aesthetic inspiration, or of sensing the incomprehensible stature of simple things, we glimpsed a great depth, which we intuit to be the hidden depths of the life we are living. We see, too, how these fleeting glimpses have occasioned within us the desire for a more abiding, daily awareness of the depths so fleetingly glimpsed. It is the grace of this desire for this abiding, daily awareness, along with all the riddles that arise in the self-transforming process of seeking to be faithful to it, that we will be referring to here as a contemplative way of life.

A contemplative way of life is a daily life imbued with contemplative experience, which is that kind of intimate, intuitive experience in which the grace of life is realized. For this reason, I will be focusing in these reflections on meditation practices and other aspects of fostering and sustaining the contemplative experience of the life we are living. But in this opening chapter, attention will be given to fostering a contemplative philosophy of life, by which is meant a personally embraced set of guiding principles founded upon the way life looks through the eyes of contemplative experience.

To have a philosophy of contemplative living is to have within oneself a personal sense of direction, a sense that one knows what one is about as a contemplative person. In the beginning stages of the journey this personal philosophy of contemplative living is especially helpful as an internalized source of guidance and encouragement. Then, too, in particularly dark stages of the journey, the philosophy—the internally believed set of guiding principles of the contemplative way—is there as one's rudder in the storm to stay the course even though everything seems unclear and uncertain.

Of course, this philosophy undergoes continual revision as one's contemplative self-transformation continues to deepen and unfold. Without a humble willingness to yield to a perpetual metamorphosis of one's own understanding of contemplative living, one runs the risk of becoming a contemplative fundamentalist, one who is ideologically rigid concerning one's own principles of contemplative self-transformation! But in the humble stance of holding to one's philosophy of contemplative living as an always-open-to-revision source of guidance and encouragement, the way is illumined, and one's enigmatic progress on it made more certain.

Having a contemplative philosophy is perhaps particularly important for us today because we live in a culture which is not contemplative in its fundamental ethos. In the cultural environment in which we live, an emphasis on productivity and achievement is rarely accompanied by a corresponding emphasis on the wisdom of remaining grounded in the meaning and value of our lives prior to and beyond all that we produce and achieve. Added to this is the fact that, due to the pervasive influence of culture on religious experience, faith communities in our present-day cultural milieu are likewise often lacking a contemplative ethos. In an emphasis on orthodoxy, social justice, moral ideals, devotional fervor, and other equally noble endeavors there is often a lack of a corresponding emphasis on a "be still and know that I am God" (Psalm 46:10) stance of contemplative self-transformation. Thus, it just might happen that a seeker of a more contemplative way of life who is a member of a believing community may feel as alone and unguided as the contemplative seeker who is not religious.

The philosophy of contemplative living which forms the infrastructure of these reflections consists of three interconnected principles constitutive of the way contemplative experience reveals reality to be. As such, these principles can be found, in one form or another, in Christian and non-Christian contemplative literature down through the ages. They are found in the following passage taken from the writings of Thomas Merton, who, with poetic elegance, writes:

What is serious to men is often very trivial in the sight of God. What in God might appear to us as "play" is perhaps what He Himself takes most seriously. At any rate the Lord plays and diverts himself in the garden of His creation, and if we could let go of our own obsession with what we think is the meaning of it all we might be able to hear His call and follow Him in His mysterious, cosmic dance. We do not have to go very far to catch echoes of that game, and of that dancing. When we are alone on a starlit night; when by chance we see the migrating birds descending on a grove of junipers to rest and eat; when we see children in a moment they are really children; when we know love in our own hearts; or when, like the Japanese poet Basho we hear an old frog land in a quiet pond with a solitary splash—at such times the awakening, the turning inside out of all values, the "newness," the emptiness and the purity of vision that make themselves evident, provide a glimpse of the cosmic dance.

For the world and time are the dance of the lord in emptiness. The silence of the spheres is the music of a wedding feast. The more we persist in misunderstanding the phenomena of life, the more we analyze them out into strange finalities and complex purposes of our own, the more we involve ourselves in sadness, absurdity and despair. But it does not matter very much, because no despair of ours can alter the reality of things or stain the joy of the cosmic dance which is always there. Indeed, we are in the midst of it, and it is in the midst of us, for it beats in our very blood, whether we want it to or not.

Yet the fact remains that we are invited to forget ourselves on purpose, cast our awful solemnity to the winds and join in the general dance.[1]

These reflections will proceed by way of poetically exploring a threefold philosophy of life gleaned from this passage. The first of the three principles found in this passage is what I will be referring to as *the divinity of what just is*. By this is meant the primitive intuitive knowledge, what the Christian, neo-Socratic philosopher Gabriel Marcel might call, the quiet inner assurance, that the present moment, just the way it is, is, in its deepest actuality, a manifestation of the divine. Our initial point of experiential access to the divinity of the present moment is found in our moments of spontaneous contemplative experience. In such moments we are instantaneously transformed in being awakened to the way we deep down really are, one with the way the present moment deep down really is.

A second principle alluded to by Merton in the above passage is what I will be referring to as our *ignorance of the divinity of what just is*. This ignorance is expressed in the "sadness, absurdity and despair" that follows upon our "misunderstanding the phenomena of life" by "resolving them into strange finalities of our own" cut off from the infinite unity of the ever-present divinity of now. A fundamental aspect of this ignorance, as we shall see, is our tendency to seek union with God by attempting to rise above or leave behind the domain of the ordinary in which the divine eternally embraces and sustains us. This second principle will sometimes by referred to as *homelessness* in that our ignorance leaves us homeless even as we remain, unbeknownst to us, at home. The exploration of these two principles will bring into focus the beginnings of a contemplative philosophy of life, a clarification of what life looks like through the eyes of contemplative experience. What is more, it is within a contemplative understanding of the dynamic interface of these first two principles that the practical necessity of the third principle of contemplative living begins to come into view.

This third principle is that of the necessity of setting out on a path of contemplative self-transformation along which we learn not to be so ignorant in learning to recognize and accept the ever present invitation to "join in the general dance." As we learn to "dance" we learn to live in a more abiding daily contemplative awareness of the divinity of the life we are living. We learn to come back home to ourselves as claimed by the divinity of ordinary experience—the divinity of this breath, this heartbeat, this fleeting glance of the passing stranger in the street.

This third how-to principle will be referred to as the *path of our homecoming* or more frequently, as the *path of our contemplative self-transformation*. The teachings offered here regarding this path consist of three directives which, like the threefold philosophy of which they are a part, are derived from contemplative experience itself and, as such, can be found in the literature of the Christian and non-Christian contemplative traditions down through the ages. The three directives are: Find your contemplative practice and practice it. Find your contemplative community and enter it. Find your contemplative teaching and follow it.

Monastic life as lived by Thomas Merton in his cloister can be seen as a cultural, historical embodiment of the threefold philosophy presented here with its attendant directives in contemplative self-transformation. Our task is to explore how it is possible to live in the midst of the world in a manner that embodies these principles of contemplative vision and self-transformation. Or, more precisely, our task is to explore how to live a contemplative way of life at a level that precedes the differences between monastic life and life in the world by addressing directly the manner in which we experience the immediacy of the present moment. More precisely still, our task is that of bringing to light the extent to which we are estranged from a contemplative awareness of the inherent holiness of the present moment so that, by means of this self-knowledge, we might set out on a path of self-transformation along which a more habitual contemplative awareness of the divinity of daily living might be realized. It is toward this end that we will continue in the next chapter to reflect on the threefold philosophy or vision of life introduced above, by examining in more detailed fashion the contemplatively realized principle of the divinity of what just is.

2. The Divinity of What Just Is

Learning to dance the cosmic dance—this is why we are here on this earth, living the life we are living. At least this is one way of expressing the heart's conviction concerning the need to recognize and move with the divinity manifested in the primordial rhythms of the day by day life we are living. Each chapter of this book is intended to serve as a kind of dance lesson. This is so in two respects. First, each chapter provides an opportunity for us to begin with a new configuration of images, a certain flow of words, in the cadences of which we might find ourselves intuitively moving to the rhythmic flow of the cosmic dance. And secondly, each chapter is a dance lesson in attempting to provide insight and guidance regarding some specific aspect of the journey of contemplative self-transformation.

The specific aspect of contemplative self-transformation explored in this chapter is that of the surprising nearness of the mystery we seek. Merton poetically alludes to this nearness in his mysterious utterance, "the world and time are the dance of the lord in emptiness." Here, at the very outset of our reflections, a note is struck which will reverberate throughout all that remains to be said. A direction is established which, if followed, will lead us to the realization of how it is possible to live a contemplative way of life in the midst of today's world.

This resounding note, however, remains unheard. This initial indication of how we are to travel is missed, if we read Merton's words solely from the vantage point of what we "think is the meaning of it all." Merton is not attempting to provide us with something to think about, but rather is inviting us to pause and ponder those moments when we have been unexpectedly overtaken by the unthinkable. By the unthinkable is meant that depth of presence that precedes and transcends all our opinions and conclusions, that nameless boundlessness that, for a moment at least, renders vacuous all our questions and answers. Nor is Merton in the above passage attempting to provide us with a method of meditation to serve as the means to the goal of contemplative living. For how can there be a means of reaching that which is already fully upon us, beating "in our very blood, whether we want it to or not"?

We ask "How is it possible to live a contemplative way of life in the midst of today's world?" In response we are invited back into the intimate domain of our own experience of traveling along a path of everyday life in which everything appears to be nothing more than it appears to be, when, suddenly, without warning, the ground beneath our feet is Mystery. The gossamer veil of appearances dissolves in an ever so subtle, ever so overwhelming realization that the present moment is unexplainably more than it appears to be. Without warning, we find ourselves falling into the abyss of a star-strewn sky or find our heart impaled by a child's laughter or the unexpected appearance of the beloved's face. Without warning we lose our footing in the silence broken and, in the breaking, deepened by the splash of a frog we did not know was there.

What is so extraordinary about such moments is that nothing beyond the ordinary is present. It is just a starlit sky, a child at play. It is just the primal stuff of life that has unexpectedly broken through the mesh of opinions and concerns that all too often hold us in their spell. It is just life in the immediacy of the present moment before thought begins. Here, in this unforeseen defenselessness, is granted the contemplative experience, however obscure it might be, that we are the cosmic dance of God, that the present moment, just the way it is, is already, in its deepest actuality, the fullness of union with God we seek. Here, like the wind that blows where it pleases, is granted, however fleetingly, that firestorm of wonderment, that "turning inside-out of all values" that is at once the poverty and the grandeur of the contemplative way.

God in his eternal stillness is hidden from every mortal eye. God in her eternal dancing is manifested everywhere. And we are this "dance of the Lord in emptiness." To speak thus is not to say that we are God. Nor is it to say we are not God. To speak thus is not to say anything at all that could be added to the store of what we think is the meaning of it all. Rather, to speak thus is a faltering attempt to give voice to the cosmic dance. It is to offer a kind of chant or incantation inviting us to that childlike surrender in which we discover within ourselves a forgotten wisdom of knowing that:

- The contemplative way is not that of striving for some far off goal that we may or may not attain, but rather is a way of discovering a secret hidden deep within our hearts.

- The contemplative way is not that of figuring out some obscure teaching, but is rather that of learning to see what is always before our eyes.

- The contemplative way is not that of mastering some method of meditation, but is rather that of learning not to do violence to the fragility of our waiting.

To hear words arising from the depths of contemplative consciousness is itself a contemplative experience. The words come to us like the hands of children clapping, like a flock of birds descending. The hearing of such words is an event consisting of an inner resonance with the words that are heard, a "yes, I know that of which you speak. I, too, have been wounded and healed, seized and set free by the inexpressible experience of the divinity of what just is." The inner experience of resounding with words arising from the depths of contemplative experience is a salvific event naming us as one who is already to some degree on the path of contemplative self-transformation. For we recognize only what we, in some sense, already know. We resonate with words arising from the depths only because our own self-transforming awakening to the depths is already in progress.

How can I live a more contemplative way of life in the midst of today's world? To ask the question from deep inside, out of some inarticulate longing for some unimaginable union is to taste in the very asking the very essence of the Way. We do not know what it is. In attempting to grasp it, there is nothing to grasp. In attempting to define it, there is nothing to define. But in learning to rest content with this empty-handed freedom we begin to realize that learning to live a contemplative way of life consists of learning to awaken to the divinity of the ground beneath our feet. In this awakening we begin to sense, however obscurely, that the great way is none other than the God-given boundlessness of the sheer immediacy of now.

Merton voices this contemplative awareness of the inherent holiness of the present moment by way of the metaphor of the cosmic dance. To explore this metaphor I will define a dance in the broadest terms possible as any movement repeated over and over to a rhythm. With this notion of a dance in mind, I invite you to imagine that someone is following you around with a video camera taping you twenty-four hours a day. Imagine, too, that the tape is then edited and set to music. In viewing the tape you would see the dance of your sitting down and standing up, your breathing in and breathing out, your being alone and with others, your being insightful in one moment, then confused the next, your being weak one moment, then strong the next, your being excited in one moment that your life shows signs of finally beginning to come together, then discouraged the next moment in thinking your life is as unmanageable as ever.

This dance is the ecstasy of God! The silence of the spheres is the music of a wedding feast this dance celebrates. In the actual moment of the heart's tremulous transformation into this divinity, all is self-evident, crystal clear, with no need for even the slightest question to arise. As the moment passes it leaves in its wake questions which reverberate with the silent music that spawned it: Is it possible that each time we stumble, fall and rise up again God can barely bear the bliss of it? Is it possible that she, God herself, reels from the ecstasy of it all, because she herself is the ALL our daily living embodies? Such questions seek not answers, but rather seek in the asking to draw us once again into an intimate, intuitive awakening to the ever-present cosmic dance.

To be awakened to the divinity of the one unending present moment in which our lives unfold is the grace. To be once again awakened is the grace that carries within it the riddle of our forgetfulness. The sun came up this morning. Now there is a grace. Where would the day be without it? But did we pause, even for an instant to behold the rising sun's truly real, truly precious nature? Perhaps we did, for sunrise sometimes has so much divinity in it that it is almost impossible not to catch at least a glimpse of the divinity it manifests. The sun will set tonight. Now there is a grace. Where would the night be without it? But will we pause, even for an instant, to behold the truly real, truly precious nature of day's end? Perhaps we will, for a sunset is sometimes so fraught with divinity we cannot help but to be grazed at least slightly by it's inherent holiness. But are we spending this day in the sustained grace of a wakeful, grateful groundedness in the sun's arc across the sky? Will we spend this evening's hours in a sustained, underlying sense of gratitude and reverence for the divinity of night? Probably not. Here is the riddle we need now to explore—the riddle of our ignorance in which, though awakened again and again, we forget again and again the divinity to which we are awakened.

3. Ignorance

Learning to live a more contemplative way of life in the midst of today's world—what could be more simple or more difficult? Simple because the contemplative way is the way of seeing what simply is in its transparent openness to the divine. It is the way of being who we simply are in the rhythmic simplicity of our breathing, in the sovereign simplicity in which day gives way to night and night to day.

Simple, too, is the manner of entering into this ever present Way. It consists of learning to sit and be, to slow down and settle in to the precious givenness of who we are right now, just the way we are. It consists of learning to loosen our hold on what we think is the meaning of it all in letting go of the tangled web of noise and concerns that seemingly hold us in its grasp. It consists of learning to become a contemplative person—one who spontaneously gravitates toward the depths of divinity manifested in each and every situation.

It is all so simple. And wouldn't it be wonderful if this simplicity were not so painfully elusive, so difficult to attain! Even as our hearts impel us to be who we ever have been, are, and ever shall be in the divinity of now, the longed for intimacy of the contemplative experience remains unconsummated. Somewhere, deep within, we obscurely sense that communion with the divine is already perfectly present in the hidden ground of our very longing to realize it. We sense that contemplative intimacy with the divine is already the reality of who we really are. And yet, all too often, this primitive contemplative wisdom is covered over by illusory obstacles we barely understand.

At first glance these obstacles seem to be neither illusory nor hard to understand. It is our schedule, we say. It is the press of there always being more to do than there is time to do it all in. Sometimes there is some truth to such statements. Sometimes, often in fact, the integrity of our search for a more contemplative way of life entails admitting just how out of hand our daily routine has become as we find ourselves hydroplaning over the surface of our life, being too busy to be. In this awareness we can then make some decisions to begin cutting back, to begin saying no in the face of pressures to say yes, so as to create, at least here and there, some breathing space in which to ground ourselves in the interiority of the life we are living.

Sometimes, however, circumstances are such that we, at least for now, cannot cut back. We have to continue on, for the time being, in the too-much-to-do stress of our daily projects and commitments. When such is the case, we need not simply regret our situation as we wait for better, less overburdened days. We can choose, instead, to look deeply into our situation, and, in so doing, discover in it lessons in contemplative living. A reference to monastic life will serve to further illustrate this point.

You would think that a cloistered monastery would provide safe harbor from the demands of a hectic schedule. And to some degree it does in that by its very nature monastic life has built right into it a sense of order and quiet pacing conducive to contemplative living. But my own experience in the cloister was that monastic life can, in its own way, become as hectic and pressured as life in the world.

Soon after I entered the monastery I was assigned to work at the growing barn, a large open structure with slanted concrete floors which housed hundreds of pigs. I worked at the growing barn all afternoon then came into the monastery to join the community for the chanting of Vespers, which followed afternoon work. My frustration was that, although I tried to comply with the emphasis given to the importance of coming to community prayer on time, I was, on some days, late for Vespers, because I simply could not get all the pig manure shoveled in time. I saw no way of cutting back on my work load because all the tasks assigned to me were essential to the maintenance of the barn, and the pigs seemed to be completely uninterested in even considering cutting back on their contribution to the problem. After much prayerful discernment I came to the conclusion that the only thing I could do was to shovel with integrity.

Perhaps you have found this to be true in your own life as well! On some days, no matter how fast you shovel, you simply cannot get it all shoveled in time for Vespers. Even getting away for a few days does not resolve the root of the problem because it all keeps piling up in your absence, waiting to be dealt with upon your return. Since the world seems unlikely to cooperate in stemming the flow of new tasks to be completed, it seems the only viable option is to shovel with integrity.

By shoveling with integrity I mean the art form of achieving a balance between several interfacing aspects of a contemplative way of carrying out one's daily obligations. The first aspect is that of being awake and present to the task at hand, performing it in a mindful manner expressive of one's faith in its inherent value. This first aspect is expressed in the Zen imperative "Do what you do. When you work, work; when you eat, eat." The contemplative way being explored here has nothing to do with encouraging a day-dreamy, half-present involvement in the task at hand, but rather has everything to do with learning to awaken to the already perfectly holy nature of the concrete immediacy of the present moment in which we find ourselves. If you were on an airplane racing down the runway just about to take off and you heard the pilot announce over the intercom that he was a mystic and felt a vision coming on, you no doubt would wish the pilot were not so mystical! Likewise, those who depend on us to carry out our duties in a responsible and conscientious manner are personal beacons inviting us to come to union with God, not by distancing ourselves from our daily obligations, but rather by coming to a contemplative realization of the inherent holiness of our daily obligations.

The second aspect of the art form of contemplatively carrying out one's daily obligations is doing what lies in one's power not to take on and maintain a daily schedule which does violence to oneself in simply trying to keep up with all that needs to be done. In discerning what it is about one's daily schedule that seems to be hindering the inner peace characteristic of contemplative living, it may be found that the source of the difficulties lies in the external circumstances of one's situation, which one must then do one's best to correct. Sometimes, however, it is not simply, nor even primarily, external circumstances, but rather one's own attitudes and behavior that are the primary contributing factors to one's difficulties. I have heard it said that whining is anger coming out through a very small opening. And, correspondingly, the experience of being overloaded with too much to do is, in some instances at least, due to the fact that the effort we are bringing to the situation is coming through the narrowed down opening of our own distancing and resentful attitudes toward our daily obligations.

The third aspect of the art form of being present to one's daily responsibilities is the one we will be focusing on here as being the most singularly contemplative in character. It consists first of recognizing and accepting that no matter how hard we work at removing the impairments and compromises to contemplative living, the impairments and compromises stubbornly refuse to go their way and leave us in peace. There seems to be woven into life itself a thread of unmanageability that makes the task of daily living at times messy, uncertain, and almost more than we can bear. Like a child building the proverbial sand castle in the incoming tide, we keep restoring and working on an inner composure and peace at the edge of mysterious forces that keep moving in, threatening to wash all our efforts away.

The next time you are caught in the frenetic energy of rush hour traffic it might be helpful to realize that even in monasteries there is a kind of cloistered rush hour, with monks running around with a lot of keys on their key rings trying to get a lot of important things finished before Vespers. The riddle is that in actuality there is no ontology to rush hour, either in the cloister or out here "in the world." God never said, "Let there be rush hour." And yet it is in the vortex of this unreality that we find ourselves.

By using the term rush hour in this manner I obviously am not referring to the phenomenon of over-crowded highways. Rather, I am referring to the log jam in which we find ourselves frustrated in our efforts to move on as quickly and efficiently as we would like, in getting done on time all that needs to be done, so that we can get up tomorrow and do it all again. In the energy field of this rush hour within our hearts there is a tendency never to pull over to the side of the road long enough to become present to the situation as a riddle to be faced and entered into with quiet, open-eyed resolve.

It is in our willingness to stop and gaze deeply into the unmanageable, loose ends dimensions of our daily living that the contemplative question comes into view—how to engage contemplatively in the dilemma of how difficult it is to live contemplatively. This means to see and understand that we need not limit ourselves to simply regretting our difficulties in contemplative living, nor to devising strategies to overcome them. For we can choose as well to gaze deeply into these difficulties as so many opportunities for us to understand ourselves as manifestations of the divine seeking union with the divine.

The more we become consciously present to our difficulty in being consciously present, the more present the difficulty becomes. We begin to see how the problem extends far beyond the context of our schedules into a generalized depth avoidance. Being at home alone in the evenings we see how, instead of sitting with the aloneness in silence, facing all that arises in the emptiness of night, we trade off this contemplative encounter with transcendence for a tray of brownies or some television shows. Being with the beloved in the evening, we see how we avoid getting vulnerable by openly sharing that which in the sharing would occasion a contemplative encounter with the depths in which two discover once again they are one. We see how, in being with the beloved in the evening, we maintain this avoidance of the depths by talking about our schedule or some other safe subject that maintains the distance that is the pain of the yet-to-be risked intimacy we long to realize. We see how the desire to be more faithful to a daily meditation practice is left unfulfilled in seemingly endless postponement. Or we see how we move in meditation from distraction to distraction, somehow unable to find, somehow skillfully avoiding, that place of falling off into the depths.

Becoming aware of how unaware we tend to be of the grace of the present moment, pausing to ponder our tendency not to pause and ponder, we enter into a state of what we might call *enlightened ignorance*. In unenlightened ignorance we do not know that we do not know. We go from project to project, from concern to concern, rarely, if ever, intentionally pausing to ask what it is that gives enduring value and meaning to our life prior to and beyond all our projects and concerns. Concerning this unenlightened ignorance I have nothing to say because all of us, insofar as we have passed over into enlightened ignorance, know all too well the dead end vacuum that a life of unenlightened ignorance entails. In the grace of *enlightened ignorance* we know we do not know. And in beginning to know that we do not know, we come upon a way of knowing grounded in humility and filled with the mysterious potential of contemplative self-transformation.

In our enlightened ignorance we see how we keep moving in and out of our awareness of the all encompassing depths each and every moment manifests. This now aware, now unaware movement is ever close at hand. It could come upon you in the reading of this book. You might be sitting right now in the confined, surface awareness of all that you agree with or all that you disagree with, of all that you understand or all that you do not understand concerning all that you are reading here. Then you may begin to realize that what you are reading here is gently seducing you away from all such considerations into a quiet vulnerability to the depths of the moment in which you find yourself. Allowing this thread of words traced out on this page to lead you to this vulnerability, you stop reading. Growing silent, you hear the sweet, abyss-like nature of your breath. Looking down you gaze into the depths of Presence manifested in and as your hands holding this book. Turning to look out the window, your heart is conquered by a lone cloud hanging in an empty sky. Suddenly you are awakened to a simple, childlike experience of the depths of divinity revealed in simply hearing, simply seeing, what simply is. Then, you begin to read on, not as a way of interrupting your contemplative groundedness in the present moment, but rather as a way of allowing your contemplative awareness to illumine the words, as the words illumine your contemplative experience. Then this stance of slow, prayerful reading gives way to the pressured need to finish this book so as to get on to reading the next book, or whatever it is that comes next in the sequence of tasks to be completed.

This now aware, now unaware movement to which we are subject would not be so relevant were it not for the fact that unless some decisive steps are taken we can end up spending almost all our days in varying degrees of unawareness in which we end up doing all sorts of foolish, hurtful things. Then we beat ourselves up for the foolish, hurtful things we have done only to repeat them again. It is almost as if we needed some ritual of self-abuse to pass the time and for which to chastise ourselves as an obsessive diversion masking what deep down we know to be our real foolishness—our persistent flight from becoming truly vulnerable to the depths of the moment-by-moment mystery of the life we are living.

In our enlightened ignorance we begin to see the heavy toll that ignorance exacts from us and from those around us. We begin to see as well the benefits that would result from learning to live in a more sustained awareness of the divinity our life manifests. We begin to appreciate how, in learning to live in a more sustained daily contemplative awareness of the life we are living, we might be sad as an appropriate response to loss, but the loss would not become a gridlock of despair. We might experience varying degrees of fear in the face of destructive or potentially destructive situations, but the fear would have no tyranny over us. We might come to a realistic awareness of some very real personal limitations, but our self-esteem would not be hanging in the balance of overcoming or hiding these limitations from ourselves or others. We might enjoy the relaxing effects of alcohol, but we would not use it to numb ourselves into an addictive cycle of self-diminishment. We would still face instances of social injustice, but we would not passively tolerate them, so moved would we be to obey the inner imperative to put ourselves on the line in every instance in which violence is done to the contemplatively realized inherent holiness of our own life and the lives of those around us.

This is not to suggest that fostering and grounding ourselves in a more contemplative awareness of the present moment is, in and of itself, enough to remedy the ills of life, as evidenced by the fact that some pretty enlightened people can do some pretty unenlightened things. Enlightened or unenlightened, we remain in some ways and in some instances subject to the cosmic dance of the sometimes glorious, sometimes senseless things that we as human beings do. Enlightened ignorance is not then the naive assumption that if only we could be awakened to life's divinity all would be well. Rather, it is the sobering realization that in our unawareness we miss out on the qualitative richness of our daily life as we live on the surface of the depths each and every moment manifests. It is the realization that our actions and attitudes expressive of this unawareness continue to perpetuate the suffering from which we seek to free ourselves.

Here we see how it is that the obstacle contemplatively pondered becomes the transcendence of the obstacle. As the humbling wisdom of enlightened ignorance grows within us, the seeker's question forms on our lips as the beginning impetus to the path of self-transformation that lies ahead. We ask, "How am I to learn to live in a more daily, abiding awareness of the inherent holiness of the life I am living?" The inner necessity and intimacy of the asking marks us as seekers of the contemplative way. And in the asking we, at some level, already know what we need to do. We need to foster in our daily living what was referred to above as the first two aspects of the art form of a contemplative approach to the demands of daily living. That is, we need to cultivate an attitude of mindfulness of the task at hand. And, in order for our efforts in mindfulness to be effective, we must learn to recognize and take steps to remedy the ways in which we become too stressed to live mindfully in the present moment. We know, too, that these two guidelines tend to remain but wishful thinking unless we faithfully set aside some daily quiet time for meditation or some other contemplative practice in which to ground ourselves in the contemplative experience of the present moment.

As important and helpful as this practical approach is, it, all by itself, suffers from two fundamental shortcomings. The first is that it tends not to work. Sooner or later (usually sooner), our plan for contemplative living leads us directly into all the obstacles, within and without, which undermine our efforts. Those of us who have been on this contemplative journey for very long know full well how ineffective our plans for contemplative living tend to be. We can look back over our shoulder to see a trail of abandoned spiritualities, like so many cars that have run out gas. Each, for an enthusiastic moment, seeming to be the long awaited point of arrival. Each leaving us, all too quickly, once again a malcontent in discovering ourselves to be, even after all our efforts, our plain old distracted self.

But the realization of the extent to which our path seems to be paved with the shards of enthusiastic beginnings come to naught is not the only shortcoming to be faced. For there is, as well, the shortcoming of self-absorption. If we are not careful our efforts to commit ourselves to living a more contemplative way of life become suspiciously limited to an exclusionary process of attempting to rise above or leave behind all that is broken and lost within ourselves and others. In such an approach our very efforts to overcome our ignorance become sublimated variations of the ignorance we are attempting to overcome.

This sad tale of our own misguided efforts needs not, however, be seen as regrettable, provided that we use our experience as an opportunity to enter into what we have referred to as the third aspect of the art form of contemplative living—namely, learning to engage contemplatively in the dilemma of how difficult it is to live contemplatively. Here is a more generous, more robust approach to the dilemma of our ignorance. This more generous approach consists, not of attempts to overcome our ignorance, but rather of a willingness to gaze deeply into it, learning its ways as we learn to get up with it in the morning and go to bed with it at night. The tonality of this approach is not about methods of attainment but is the tonality of a willingness to see and accept the dark divinity of our plight of being trapped on the outer circumference of the inner richness of the life we are living.

In this humble self-knowledge there is the growing realization that this whole journey of contemplative self-transformation is not simply or primarily about "me" in my private quest for inner peace. Rather it is about entering into the homelessness of the whole world being uniquely expressed in my experience of it. Likewise, we begin to discover that the journey on which we find ourselves is not one of rising above or leaving behind our unaware self. Rather, the journey consists of waking up and coming home to the divinity at once hidden and revealed in the dance of the now so near now so far away, the now so noble now so Oh-my-God-what-have-I-done stuff of our own life and the lives of those around us.

Homelessness—how we fear the pain of it, even as we feel its inevitability in our own life and in the lives of those around us! The human drama of homelessness takes many forms, wears many faces: psychological disturbances in which we are no longer at home in the intimacy of our own lived experience; a troubled marriage in which no dwelling can be found in a relationship we assumed would always prevail; a crisis of faith in which our religious tradition since childhood ceases to be what we deep down have come to believe, or at least its truths are no longer true for us in the way they used to be true for us; a series of illnesses in which our body is no longer the home we have known it to be; the final, inevitable homelessness of death. It is a homelessness so boundless that the never questioned assurance of tomorrow's sunrise no longer shelters us.

In Southern California where I live there are many street people; they are homeless in the literal sense. Once, while walking from my car to my psychotherapy office, I looked up to see coming toward me a woman in desperate straits. She was obviously homeless in more ways than one. Her tousled hair was matted with dirt as was her ill shaped tent of a dress. Even at some distance I could tell by the look in her eye that she was somewhere else, having been carried off by God knows what—mental illness? substance abuse? too many losses too painful to endure? With one hand she pushed a grocery cart brimming over with the tattered edges of all her belongings. In the other hand—and this is what most singularly struck me about her—she carried a dome shaped bird cage, in which there flitted about the small iridescent jewel of a bird. A finch, I think. And it struck me: the bird is her soul—a jewel caged in the ravages of homelessness. We walked past each other saying nothing. Feeling the tug and pull of the conflicting emotions I always feel in these non-encounters, I continued on. I did not look back, but carried her somehow inside of me, in the way we carry those whom we encounter in some manner that we know matters very much, but which we cannot as yet understand.

I continued up the street to my psychotherapy office, where I sat all day long as each therapy client came in, one after the other, each sitting across from me on my large teal green leather sofa. Each was a well groomed, middle class, upper-middle class, or upper class woman or man, each coming from and returning to a home they called their own, each coming to share the painful story of their homelessness, their painful inability to dwell in a safe, nurturing way in the concreteness of their own lived experience. And I sat there in my teal green leather chair, relying on my clinical training and experience in my attempts to help each of these people. I sat there, relying even more on my own ongoing process of learning to be at home in my own homelessness, being as present as I could be to each of them, trusting that presence holds the key to a life worth living.

At a certain level all this is quite complicated. Each form of homelessness has its own origin, its own unique pain. Each calls for its own response. But from a contemplative point of view, all forms of homelessness share a common origin, which is our estrangement from the contemplative experience of the life we are living. What are we to do? What kind of response is adequate to such a dilemma? Learn to meditate? Cultivate attitudes of contemplative wakefulness? Recognize, accept, and work through all the ways we flee from, compromise and do violence to ourselves and others? Yes, all these things are responses to the dilemma of our homelessness, our being so unaware of the inherent holiness of the life we are living. But, all these efforts become themselves perpetrators of ignorance unless they become embodiments of a humble recognition of ourselves as we really are. This humble recognition brings us to a fork in the road, where we either despair or go deeper. To despair is to die inside, to lose all hope of ever being the person whom we deep down know ourselves to be in the intimacies of our own moments of spontaneous contemplative experience. To go deeper is the work of love, particularly the love of compassion, which freely lets go of our hard fought for levels of imagined holiness and serenity to identify with the preciousness of ourselves and others, still homeless and lost in the ravages of ignorance.

This is not to say that the whole of the contemplative path can be reduced to love, for the path can be reduced to nothing. Rather it is to say that unless the path is grounded in compassionate love, nothing real or lasting comes of it. Unless our efforts in contemplative living embody this compassionate identification with the preciousness of ourselves and others lost in ignorance, our imagined path of contemplative self-transformation tends to be but a sublimated cul-de-sac, a closed loop that leads nowhere except back to the estrangement from which we are trying to free ourselves. It is toward the path of contemplative self-transformation grounded in compassion that we now turn our attention, beginning with the first directive: Find your contemplative practice and practice it.

PART TWO:

FIND YOUR CONTEMPLATIVE PRACTICE AND PRACTICE IT

4. Discovering Your Contemplative Practices

We are in the midst of exploring the path of self-transformation along which we learn to become the contemplative person we deep down really are and long to be. So far, we have been emphasizing the vision dimension of this transformation, suggesting that a contemplative person is one who has a contemplative vision or philosophy of life. This vision or philosophy, as we have seen, grounds itself in a faith in the revelatory nature of our moments of spontaneous contemplative experience as disclosing to us the inherently holy nature of the present moment. As we learn to establish ourselves in this founding first principle of life's essential holiness, the second principle comes into view as our tendency not to see the divinity of the life we are living. As we learn to live with this awareness of our unawareness we discover that the obstacle, contemplatively pondered, becomes the path along which we are transformed. For our awareness of our unawareness draws us into the third principle, which is that of the felt need to commit ourselves to a path of self-transformation along which we become more habitually aware of and responsive to the inherent holiness of life.

This path of self-transformation can be expressed and explored in three directives: Find your contemplative practice and practice it. Find your contemplative community and enter it. Find your contemplative teaching and follow it. We begin here with the first of these three directives: Find your contemplative practice and practice it.

A contemplative practice is any act, habitually entered into with your whole heart, as a way of awakening, deepening, and sustaining a contemplative experience of the inherent holiness of the present moment. Your practice might be some form of meditation, such as sitting motionless in silence, attentive and awake to the abyss-like nature of each breath. Your practice might be simple, heartfelt prayer, slowly reading the scriptures, gardening, baking bread, writing or reading poetry, drawing or painting, or perhaps running or taking long, slow walks to no place in particular. Your practice may be to be alone, really alone, without any addictive props and diversions. Or your practice may be that of being with that person in whose presence you are called to a deeper place. The critical factor is not so much what the practice is in its externals as the extent to which the practice incarnates an utterly sincere stance of awakening and surrendering to the Godly nature of the present moment.

At any given time we are likely to have not a single practice but rather a constellation of practices, often with one of them as our primary practice. Others may surround it, each carrying its own special place in our life. Thus, we might have as our primary practice some form of meditation while also experiencing the importance of spiritual reading, liturgical prayer, and preparing meals with a mindful, reverential stance of awareness of the eucharistic nature of every meal. As the months and years go by the constellation changes. New practices emerge. Practices that have been present for years fall out of the picture. And the ones that stay on undergo a series of subtle but far-reaching transformations.

There is an oblique and diffused quality to contemplative practices as I am speaking of them here. We may, in fact, engage in these activities for quite some time without consciously thinking of them as contemplative practices. But upon reflection we are able to see how these simple acts serve to ground us in a simple, child-like awareness of that which is truly real and precious in the life we are living. We discover by experience that if we are faithful to our contemplative practices our practices faithfully lead us in the direction of a more daily, abiding awareness of the divinity of the life we are living.

If we are not careful, however, the demands of each day's events easily drown out the unassuming importance of fidelity to those simple acts that intimately awaken us to the ultimate meaning and value of those same daily events. Remaining faithful to our contemplative practices calls for the integrity of remaining faithful to a commitment that nobody sees; it consists of giving ourselves over with all our heart to simple acts which, on the surface, seem to be but the incidental passage of time. But if we are faithful to this unassuming path of fidelity to our daily contemplative practices, the subtle awareness of the depths to which they grant access begins to permeate the very texture of our daily experience of living. Slowly, almost imperceptibly at first, fidelity to our contemplative practices evolves into an habitual awareness that does not miss the surprise appearance of God showing up in something as immediate and simple as the sunlight that suddenly fills a room on a cloudy day.

Finding your contemplative practice is then an event that occurs in each and every granting of contemplative experience in which the divinity of the present moment is realized. Flowing out from each finding is the possibility of then learning to *practice* your contemplative practice by learning to "hang out in the neighborhood" where the granting of spontaneous contemplative experience of the moment occurred. If the granting of the contemplative experience of the depths occurs in turning to see a flock of birds descending, then, in the contemplative beholding of birds, you have found your practice, to which you can quietly commit yourself in an ongoing process of learning to see and take to heart the divinity of birds. If the granting of the contemplative experience of the depths occurs in a moment of knowing love in your own heart, then in love you have found your practice, which you can then faithfully practice in a lifelong process of learning to be vulnerable to each new visitation of love. So it is that ever since that night long ago when your heart was smitten by the moon's divinity, you, out of some inner necessity of your heart, see to it that you are available for occasional, little, wordless rendezvous with the moon. Sitting in the glow of her primitive light, quietly beholding the depths of divinity that light discloses, you practice your practice. By such fidelities you, without your knowing how, are led along the path of your transformation into the depths of divinity that your daily living manifests.

Each arena of self-transformation has its own modalities of contemplative awakening and its own corresponding contemplative practices. Marital love, for example, is an arena of self-transformation that clearly has its moments of spontaneous contemplative experience in which husband and wife realize, in an intimate, intuitive, body-grounded manner, a oneness that never ends. The granting of this experience may occur in the naked embrace of sexual intercourse. When this is so, penetration and orgasm are realized to be not simply physiological processes, but, what is more, ways of yielding over their last defense against the free fall in which there is nothing for them to hold on to except one another. Or the contemplative experience of love's overflowing nature may be granted in times of crisis, in which one is there for the other at a tremendous cost to oneself. These and all similar moments of spontaneous contemplative experience occur in marriage of their own accord as moments integral to the serendipitous nature of love.

The couple committed to intimacy does not, however, leave intimacy to chance. This is especially so as each one experiences the toll that daily pressures and the baggage of woundedness that each has brought into the marriage can take on their intimacy. But if all goes well, if they are cooperative with love's ways, they learn to recognize and faithfully give themselves over to those acts, which they discover by experience are inherently endowed with the capacity to awaken and deepen their love. They take long slow walks together, or they sit sharing what most needs to be shared, or they take off their clothes, make love, and in the afterglow find themselves to be once again in the depths in which they are one. Or they may pray together, or simply sit in a mutual silence in which each gives witness to the other of love's ultimately unspeakable nature. They are, in short, faithful to those simple acts which they discover by experience are inherently endowed with the capacity to awaken, deepen, and sustain a contemplative awareness of love's never ending ways.

The self-transforming process just observed in marital love can be observed as well in religious faith, being in the midst of nature, art, poetry, solitude, social justice, philosophical reflection, the healing of psychological wounds, and all other arenas of fundamental human experience. Each of these arenas form the context in which we are, from time to time, awakened in an intimate, intuitive, body-grounded manner to the depths of divinity that daily living manifests. And each of these arenas provides as well its own practices in which moments of contemplative awakening evolve into an habitual contemplative awareness of the divinity of daily living.

5. Meditation

Meditation is a contemplative practice that is particularly stark, simple and direct in its capacity to awaken, deepen and sustain the contemplative experience of the divinity of the present moment. In introducing the topic of meditation, it seems most natural for me to write as if I were actually speaking to you personally as a beginner who asked for some introductory guidelines in how to meditate. This will allow me to speak in the direct, how-to language proper to the actual experience of meditation practice.

In using this prescriptive language, however, I am assuming that as you read these guidelines you are discerning the manner in which they apply to you. For various reasons you may not be drawn to meditation practice, or you may have tried meditation and found it not be among the contemplative practices that are suited to your particular temperament or needs. Even so, you might find that much of what is contained in this exploration of meditation does apply to you. For the emphasis will not be on meditation as such, but rather on the contemplatively realized unitive world that we as seekers of a more contemplative way of life seek to enter, regardless of what our particular practices might be.

An analogy can be made to reading a set of guidelines for backpacking in Yosemite National Park. While the guidelines in some of their specifics would clearly be most useful to those planning to backpack in Yosemite, some of the hints and suggestions might prove to be quite helpful to those planning to backpack anywhere. On a broader scale still, the guidelines might be enjoyable reading for those who simply appreciate and enjoy being in the midst of nature. In similar fashion, you might find that, although meditation is not among your contemplative practices, reading about meditation practice is itself a kind of contemplative practice in which you can discover insights into the nature of the contemplative experience that obliquely graces your reading, your quiet walks, or whatever your contemplative practices might be.

Or it may be that you are quite drawn to meditation and are already underway in learning a particular method of meditation which may vary in some respects from the guidelines given here. In that case you can focus on those aspects of meditation presented here which may apply to your particular practice. Yet another possibility is that you have been meditating for many years in a manner quite similar to the guidelines being proposed here. The intended focus here is not on the specifics of the method presented, but rather on the never to be exhausted fundamentals of self-transformation that all contemplative practices and all methods of meditation in particular tend, with God's grace, to evoke.

The guidelines for meditation which we will be exploring are these: With respect to the body: sit still, sit straight, hands in a comfortable or meaningful position in your lap, eyes closed or lowed toward the ground, slow, deep natural breathing; with respect to the mind: be present, open, and awake, neither clinging to nor rejecting anything; and with respect to attitude: non-judgmental compassion toward yourself as you discover yourself clinging to and rejecting everything, nonjudgmental compassion toward others whose powerlessness is one with yours.

These guidelines for meditation consist of some of the basic rudiments of the Buddhist meditation traditions integrated with the kindred teachings of the Christian sources quoted and referred to in this book. My own understanding of the approach to meditation taken here, however, is characterized best as neither Buddhist nor Christian. For our present intention is to be true to the essence of what these traditions share in common in their genius for recognizing and distilling out those simple, archetypal acts and attitudes inherently endowed with the capacity to awaken contemplative experience prior to the point at which it breaks up into the spectrum of the various traditions in which it is realized. It is these simple, archetypal acts and attitudes that we will be poetically exploring here, beginning with the directive to sit still.

Sit Still

The first suggested guideline for meditation practice is to sit still, to move as little as possible. Sitting still is practical in that it helps to still the mind, thereby enhancing present moment attentiveness. As present moment attentiveness deepens, our sitting still becomes an act of incarnate faith, giving witness to ourselves and to the whole world that ultimately there is nowhere to go. In our ignorance we do not know that this is so. In our ignorance we attempt to apply the standards of the relative order of contingencies, with all its places to go, goals to reach, needs to be met with the ultimate order of the depths in which we sit. Having in mind some yet to be realized degree of spiritual attainment, we sit and say, with a sigh, "I wonder if I will ever get there?" As we sit, we assume our difficulties in meditating profoundly, our difficulties in living contemplatively are due to our disturbingly slow progress along a disturbingly circuitous path leading to a disturbingly distant destination.

But from a contemplative point of view, incarnate as the stillness of our meditation practice, we are not suffering because we cannot "get there," but because we find it so incredibly difficult to be here, fully present, open and awake to all this present moment really is. And why do we find present moment attentiveness to be so difficult? In part, because we are trying so hard to get there! Somebody told us back there in our childhood, back there at yesterday's ultimatum meeting, what we ourselves have come to believe—that unless we are able to "get there," finally arriving at some required degree of efficiency, compliance, virtue, holiness, or spiritual attainment, we will not be real enough or lovable enough to be, at last, in the winner's circle of the game of life. Having grown weary of this ignorance of failing to see in all we gain and lose the divinity of all we gain and lose, we now sit still.

In this stillness we learn from our body how to be. For while our mind in its restlessness is prone to lag behind and lurch ahead of the present moment, our body is always still in always bodying forth our oneness with the one unending present moment in which our lives unfold. Even in death, the body is right there in death, not leaving the present moment but rather falling into its eternal depths, disappearing from view.

It is relative to this tendency for our mind to be somewhere other than the present moment that we can more readily understand why it is often suggested that a single meditation period last for twenty to thirty minutes. This is short enough to be compassionate with respect to our limitations in stillness, and practical with respect to the demands of our schedule. At the same time it is long enough to allow us to begin to settle into the felt sense of our bodily presence in the present moment. The contemplative experience of the felt sense of one's bodily presence in the present moment is often so subtle that it can begin and continue for quite some time without our being consciously aware of it. But if we are sincere and quietly patient in our whole-hearted intention of simply sitting still, the noise of our customary preoccupations and concerns begins to fall away. In this quiet clearing the contemplative experience of the felt sense of one's bodily presence in the present moment can begin to slowly appear. As if waking from a dream, as if falling backwards in slow motion into the luminous depths of who we simply are—one with all the present moment simply is—we are born into a full statured stillness beyond our own reckoning.

Fortunately for us, even before we sit to meditate for the first time, we already know something of the full statured stillness of our awakened bodily presence in the present moment. This is so because our moments of spontaneous contemplative experience grant this full statured stillness to us. In the instant of our turning to see a flock of birds descending, or of knowing love in our own heart, we are stilled in being deeply moved by the depths of the immediately arising grace of birds descending, the immediately arising grace of love arising. Whether the awe arises suddenly or comes upon us slowly, almost imperceptibly, like water filling the marshlands, there is the felt sense of there being no place to go. All we could ever hope or long for is somehow hidden, somehow obscurely manifested in this present moment. As the moment of contemplative encounter with the depths begins to dissipate, we linger wordlessly about the scene, still held in the aura of the awe that envelops us. We move on to the task that awaits us, leaving the birds to themselves, leaving the still darkening horizon, or the beloved's touch, or the moment of childlike prayer, not with a sense of having fully entered into the depths obscurely experienced there, but, to the contrary, with the conviction that we had hardly begun to do so. We move on, intuitively knowing that even if we would stay forever, we would never exhaust the contemplatively sensed inexhaustibility to which the moment fleetingly granted access.

When we sit in meditation, we sit with a heart pregnant with faith in the revelatory nature of our moments of spontaneous contemplative experience disclosing to us the divinity of the ceaseless flow of the one, ever-present, present moment in which we sit. Our fidelity to the stillness of our practice is the labor that gives birth to our awakened bodily presence in the present moment bodying forth the mystery that we seek. This labor has an intentional dimension, in that our sitting still embodies our intention of being awakened to and transformed in the divinity of the present moment. This intentional element, however, must itself be transformed in the stillness our sitting still embodies. For if we are not careful our intention to sit still turns present moment attentiveness into another "there," which, in the midst of all our fidgeting, we hope to "get to." This purification of the intention to sit still occurs of its own accord as we simply sit still, moving as little as possible, letting all self-imposed shoulds fall away, accepting ourselves as we are in the immediacy of the present moment before thought begins.

When we sit to meditate we do not think such thoughts about stillness, for in our meditation we do not think of anything at all, but rather we let go of our customary reliance on thinking in being present, open and awake, neither clinging to nor rejecting anything. But such thoughts can help us to enter into our sitting still with an intuitive appreciation of sitting still as a path of self-transformation. Such thoughts can help deepen our faith in simply sitting still as a point of entry into the depths in which we are intimately awakened to our bodily presence presencing forth the unmanifested presence we call God.

As we learn to enter into the full statured stillness of our meditation practice, we begin to sense the importance of discerning a practical question: "What should I do when my nose starts to itch or my foot starts to hurt?" The question is not all that relevant with respect to the little itch or hurt that is just passing through at the periphery of our awareness. Rather, the full relevance of the question comes to the fore with the great-big, decided-to-move-in, take-over-and-stay-awhile itch or hurt. What then? Sometimes, what is best is simply to scratch your nose or to move your foot slightly to a more comfortable position. This is sometimes best because it is always best to do what is most natural, most truly grounded in the universal dignity of ordinary human experience.

Sometimes, however, what is most natural in fidelity to the wisdom of a higher order of contemplative experience is not to itch your nose or move your foot in the realization that the path of contemplative self-transformation entails a willingness to choose freely to enter into the mysterious domain of the impotency of choice. We possess the ability to choose to remove ourselves and others from painful and distressful situations. By actualizing this ability we fulfill our moral responsibility toward ourselves and others. But if we are always leaping in, fixing the situation—immediately scratching what itches, moving what hurts—our practice of bodily stillness never ripens. Our practice is never allowed to carry us all the way home to the hallowed clearing where our lives all converge in the impotency of our will to change all that we are powerless to change.

The stillness of our meditation practice begins to ripen as we, instead of scratching what itches or moving slightly a foot or hand that has become uncomfortable, choose instead to remain still in a willingness to enter into the stillness of those who are physically paralyzed or otherwise unable to move. I say "otherwise unable to move" to extend immobility to include any time any of us are unable to move beyond a painful, distressful situation: the ending of a relationship, losing one's job or one's home, becoming ill, growing old, or realizing that one's own death draws near. Such moments are risky. They can break our spirit, causing us to give up, to assume the stance of the helpless victim or the addict who attempts to overcome the pain of the moment by numbing his or her experience of what is really happening. While not without risk, such instances of being stilled can occasion a falling into the depths in which wisdom is granted to those transformed in the paradoxical power of powerlessness deeply accepted.

It is into these paradoxical depths that we are invited to enter in the stillness of our practice, by not scratching our itching nose, not moving our hurting foot, not stopping our meditation simply because we are sleepy, distracted, or discouraged. I once attended a six day Christian-Zen retreat conducted by Rev. Hans Koenen, a Jesuit priest from the Netherlands. We were all in silence, sitting still in meditation six to eight hours a day. That much stillness can cause a considerable amount of bodily pain, which in the silent stillness of the practice becomes itself a mystery beyond fathoming. Each day Rev. Koenen presided at liturgy in the meditation hall. When the time came for communion, he passed the consecrated bread and then passed the chalice of consecrated wine saying, "Drink this cup which contains the suffering of the whole world." When I put the chalice to my lips, tears flowed from the awareness that the pain in my back and shoulders from the long hours of meditation, while truly mine, was not just mine but was rather, in some inscrutable manner, one with the pain of all those meditating with me in the communal stillness of our practice. Beyond this was the realization that our communal pain was in some way one with the pain of all people everywhere in their moments of being powerless to free themselves from painful and distressful situations. Drinking the cup is recognized in such circumstances to be a communal celebration of powerlessness not as a cul-de-sac of hopelessness, but as a point of entry into a freedom and expansiveness that circumstances are powerless to contain. In Christian faith the cross is the great sign of this inscrutable freedom that our sitting still lays bare. This freedom is not a freedom over all constraints, but a freedom that remains unimpeded in the midst of all constraints.

We vary greatly from one another in our ability to actualize our potential to free ourselves and others from painful and life-threatening situations. This is why we need each other; those more capable can help those who are less capable. But we are all one in our common destiny of finding ourselves at that place in which our God-given ability to relieve suffering, to make things better, gives way to the divinity of our powerlessness to change, by brute force of our will, the situation in which we find ourselves. Here is where we either despair or go deeper. Despair is the outcome of having placed all our hope in our now impotent ability to make things turn out the way we think they need to turn out. To go deeper is to drink the cup of our common destiny in which divinity flows unimpeded through our communal powerlessness.

Perhaps it all comes down to this—by the stillness of our practice, not moving that which hurts, not scratching what itches, we enter into the mysterious domain where we all belong to each other as one in our common lot of finding ourselves powerless to free ourselves from that which has befallen us. And here, where we all belong to each other, is where we most radically belong to God who enigmatically sustains us in our powerlessness to sustain ourselves. To speak in this manner is not to claim being delivered from our desolation, but rather to give witness to being delivered from the delusion that our moments of desolation have any ultimate power over us. It is to give witness to the self-transforming realization of being transformed in desolation, such that we come to discover in it the divinity beyond gain and loss.

In the Psalms (46:10) God gently commands the attentive believer, "Be still and know I am God." Here, expressed in religious language, is a yet broader and richer understanding of stillness being a way to divine knowledge. The direct relevance of this text to our current concern of stillness in meditation practice was brought home to me in my participation in a group meditation led by Rev. Thomas Hand, a Jesuit priest on staff at Mercy Center, a retreat house in Burlingame, California. He began the group meditation experience by asking all present to repeat after him the psalm verse, "Be still and know I am God." After we did so, he continued, having us repeat the verse after him, as he shortened it each time, "Be still and know I am. . . . Be still and know. . . . Be still. . . . Be." This intonation of a scripture text distilled down to the black hole of a naked "BE" was immediately echoed by the ringing of a bell, the resonance of which, in becoming silent, left us in the communal stillness of meditation.

I have since used this method in leading my own group meditation sessions. For here, it seems to me, is a contemplative liturgy of the word disclosing the fecund meeting place where words lead to and drop off into a great stillness of the mind awakened to and lost in a Presence beyond words. Perhaps it is in this meeting place that scripture becomes most truly God's word, that poetry and prophecy and the intimate utterance reveal to us the power of a word to translate us into the silent, attentive depths from which such words arise. Similarly, we can say that here is a liturgy of the word in which seekers of a more contemplative way of life gather to celebrate the present moment as a divine activity ceaselessly arising out of a divine stillness to which it ceaselessly returns.

And so if you meditate every day for thirty minutes, sit still with all your heart every day for thirty minutes.

If you meditate every day for thirty minutes until death, sit still with all your heart every day for thirty minutes until death. For the stillness of our practice is a stillness unto death. The stillness of our practice is, in truth, the stillness of death itself, which, as our faith assures us, is not simply a termination, but a termination that is as well a gateless barrier[1] through which we forever pass into God.

Sit Straight

The next suggested guideline for meditation practice is to sit straight. When giving meditation-intensive retreats, I will look down the rows of those sitting in meditation to see many of the participants are not sitting straight, but rather are sitting with their back and shoulders slumped slightly forward and their head bent slightly downward. Seeing them helps me to renew the straightness of my posture. Present moment attentiveness is enhanced not by slumping forward but rather by sitting with one's spine, neck and head straight, with one's ears in a vertical line with one's shoulders, not tense or rigid but relaxed and solidly grounded in the center of one's gravity.

In the Zen Buddhist tradition, one meditates sitting crossed legged on a small, firm cushion called a *zafu*, which, when properly used, facilitates sitting straight and firmly grounded in the stillness of the practice. If you have the physical agility and inclination to try using a cushion there are a number of introductory books on Buddhist meditation methods containing photographs or drawings demonstrating the various ways to use the cushion. Or better yet, if you have the opportunity to do so, you can visit a Buddhist meditation community to learn first hand the proper use of the cushion. Similar to the cushion in its effectiveness in promoting a straight posture during meditation, is the use of a small bench that one uses by kneeling on the floor, placing the bench across the back of one's calves then lowering one's self onto the bench. I have seen these benches used and sold at a number of Christian retreat houses throughout the United States and Canada. You are likely to find, however, that it is most natural to sit in a chair that is firm, with a straight supporting back and which is neither too high nor too low for you, with both feet flat on the ground, and your spine straight. Besides being what is most likely to feel most comfortable and most natural, meditating in a chair has the distinct advantage of establishing our meditation practice firmly in our own culture.

Sitting straight is practical in that it enhances present moment attentiveness, particularly with respect to a sequence of events integral to our entering into the meditative state. We sit still. As we become still we become relaxed. As we become relaxed there is a natural tendency for our head to begin drooping slightly forward and to slip off into sleepiness or daydreaming. Our sitting straight enters this sequence of events as the dynamic counter point at which our drifting toward a sleepy, dreamy, unawareness becomes instead a state of being wide awake and deeply relaxed at once. Each time sleepiness, daydreaming, or slumping begins to overtake us, we renew our alertness by renewing the straightness of our posture, *being careful in doing so not to disturb the deepening relaxation of our bodily stillness*. With the whole self still and quiet, as if about to fall asleep, yet remaining in the wakefulness our sitting straight embodies, we move into the meditative state of sustained bodily wakefulness to the divinity of the present moment in which we sit.

The body-grounded wakefulness our sitting straight embodies passes through different states or, we might say, seasons, each with its own grace and its own lessons concerning the path of our contemplative self-transformation. At times the dynamics of sustained body wakefulness is maintained in the season of quiet vigilance. Sitting rested and alert, we are able, in almost effortless fashion, to notice and correct the first beginnings of each little instance of starting to slump forward or drifting toward sleepiness. These little corrective moves can be compared to driving a car in a straight line toward a distant point on the horizon. The car continues to travel forward in a straight line only because the driver senses and corrects each small instance of the car drifting to the left or right. In similar fashion, as we sit in meditation we arrive at our destination by vigilantly correcting each small, subtle, drifting away from sustained bodily wakefulness. The difference is that in meditation the destination is not "out there" as some great distance ahead of us. Rather, the destination is that of our awakening to God, manifested in and as our sitting still and straight in the one unending present moment in which our lives unfold.

At other times the body-grounded wakefulness our sitting straight embodies is an arduous struggle to simply stay awake. You do not need to experience this struggle with sleepiness for very long to appreciate the practicality of meditating when you are not so exhausted that you can barely stay awake or so distracted that you are continually drifting off into your preoccupations with the burdens of the day. When sleepiness is too much to resist, it is sometimes best to follow the common sense route of cutting short the meditation session to engage in a more active contemplative practice, such as meditative walking or spiritual reading, in which it is easier to stay awake. At still other times what is best is to listen to what your body is telling you and go to bed for some badly needed sleep.

Sometimes, however, there may be the intuitive sense that even though you are struggling with sleepiness and daydreaming, it is important to continue meditating. As you know, if you have meditated very much at all, some of the biggest breakthroughs can come in the midst of great struggle. A fog bank of sleepiness and daydreaming can suddenly give way to an inner clarity and depth you would not have reached had the meditation been cut short. Learning to trust your intuitive sense of when to stop and when to continue meditating in periods of great sleepiness and daydreaming is part of the maturation process of learning to know and trust what is required in being faithful to one's evolving contemplative self-transformation. It is worth noting that it is in times of struggle and hardship that we can appreciate the benefit of meditating in a group, in which each one present draws from and contributes to the communal resolve to continue on in fidelity to the practice.

Regardless of how arduous meditation may become, what is most important is to keep in mind that the relationship of wakefulness to sleepiness and daydreaming in effective meditation is never adversarial, but always dynamically reciprocal. To see how this is so, an analogy can be made to the non-adversial reciprocity between awareness and non-awareness in an intimate relationship. Each time two people in a healthy intimate relationship drift away from intimacy, each takes the responsibility to be honest and vulnerable in talking about what is happening. In these talks all kinds of feelings come up as things hard to say and hear are said and heard. But, if the couple stays on course, all this messy stuff proves to be the way they, in the intimate sharings of their drifting from intimacy, discover greater intimacy.

In the enlightened ignorance of being aware of their unawareness, they learn to keep calling each other to awareness as a vital aspect of the work of love. Similarly, we enter into bodily wakefulness of our oneness with God in the present moment not by never drifting off into sleepiness or daydreaming, but rather by the work of love in which, each time we drift off into sleepiness or daydreaming, we renew our wakefulness by once again renewing our conscious awareness of sitting straight. Sitting thus, lovingly accepting ourselves as we are, we are transformed in a body-grounded compassionate awareness of the divinity of ourselves in our fragility.

There is also the season of experiencing all sorts of emotional stirrings in meditation. Sitting still and straight we make our descent into the depths of divinity that the present moment manifests. The descent does not detour around but rather passes directly through all that lies within. So it is that as we sit still and straight, descending ever deeper, we pass through all the emotions that stir within. As if out of nowhere, may come feelings of inner peace and consolation only to give way in other times to feelings of sadness, anger, and loneliness. Our descent into the depths is impeded to the extent we cling to or reject any of these emotions. Our descent continues on, ever deeper, as we simply sit, present, open, and awake to all that appears as it appears, to all that passes away as it passes away.

The emotional stirrings that occur in meditation are sometimes continuous with deeper awakenings of contemplative experience, disclosing to us that we are not just our ego. This knowledge of being more than simply our ego is granted to us in our moments of spontaneous contemplative experience. It is given to us in our faith revealing to us that we are children of God. And it is given to us in meditation, causing us to feel happy, peaceful, and fulfilled. But to the extent we are still subject to an egocentric understanding of what it means to be more than just our ego, we foolishly imagine that meditation will empower us to be an enlightened ego, a holy ego, an ego one with God. As the poverty and emptiness of meditation continue to erode away these egocentric misconceptions, it is normal to experience sadness and anxiety. For, after all, we have become accustomed to the prison house of our delusional notions of being nothing more than who we imagine, think and feel ourselves to be. We have become attached to the confining illusions that confine us and in which we continue to suffer.

Imagine a caterpillar who is about to undergo a metamorphosis. Imagine, too, that this caterpillar has been eagerly looking forward to this great event. It has studied and researched metamorphosis. It has a camera and a journal at hand to take pictures and carefully record everything that happens, so as to publish what it senses will be a best-seller—*My Metamorphosis*. But when its metamorphosis actually begins to occur, something the caterpillar had never anticipated happens. Its brain begins to change first. That is, the state of caterpillar consciousness from which it assumed it was going to observe its metamorphosis is the first thing that begins to change! For a butterfly is not a caterpillar with wings. If it were, it could never fly. Resurrection is not the resuscitation of a corpse. Enlightenment is not insight.

We desire our transformation into God. Our meditation practice is the living embodiment of this desire. But insofar as we are still subject to identifying ourselves with an egocentric understanding of this transformation, its actual occurrence occasions a dark night in which, with fear and trembling, we learn to let go of and die to who we imagined ourselves to be. In part, the emotional stirrings of fear and anxiety experienced in mediation arise from this self-transformation process in which we must let go and die to identifying with anything less than a divine understanding of our transformation into the divine.

The season of emotional stirrings is also closely associated with remembering recent and far distant events. Suddenly remembering something sad, we feel sad. Suddenly remembering something that made us angry, we feel angry. Remembering a warm and loving moment, we feel warm and loving. What was said above regarding the flow of emotions, holds true regarding the flow of images of past events. Our descent into the depths is impeded to the extent we cling to or reject any memory that arises. Our descent continues on unimpeded as each memory is simply remembered as it arises and then simply allowed to pass as it passes away. For this passage down through all that lies within entails a willingness to remember all that has happened to us, without rejecting or identifying with anything that has happened to us. This willingness to remember is both challenging and self-transforming with respect to our memories of painful and possibly traumatizing experiences.

What many of us tend to do with painful and difficult experiences is to hide from them, by burying them away inside us, where they remain as unfelt, unacknowledged aspects of our own life. Up to a point, the capacity to repress or dissociate our painful and difficult memories is an asset, a sign of ego strength that allows us to get on with our life in the aftermath of painful and difficult experiences. It is good to know how to hide from painful things which lurk within. It is good to know how to distance ourselves from inner feelings, which if allowed to come out all at once, might flood us with painful emotions beyond what we could endure. The difficulty is, however, that our emotions are dimensions of our being. To be split off from our own feelings is to be split off from a vital dimension of being. To hide from our own feelings is to be hiding from ourselves. If we are not careful we can learn to hide so well that nobody can find us. The cheerful, capable mask we present to others becomes so opaque to what we carry within that nobody ever sees who we, deep down, really are. If we are not careful, we can learn to hide so well that we cannot find ourselves. Our undealt with, unprocessed, emotional pain and loss becomes hidden from our conscious awareness. As we continue to renew the straightness of our posture in a manner that does not disturb the deepening relaxation of the practice, we pass through this hidden storehouse of sequestered off pain and loss within ourselves.

As we sit in meditation, the sustained stance of being present, open, and awake to all that arises as it arises, to all that passes away as it passes away, is our sure guide down through all the layers of emotions and memories that lie within. In this willingness to continue on, neither clinging to nor rejecting anything, there emerges a more expansive, all encompassing sense of self. Sitting in this ongoing openness to oneself is the living embodiment of knowing and trusting that life is, in essence, benign, in spite of all the scary, hurtful stuff that has happened and will continue to happen. Infinitely more than this, sitting this way embodies a contemplatively realized oneness with God manifested in and as one's ceaselessly arising and passing away experience of the ceaselessly arising and passing away present moment.

Sitting still and straight in meditation, we feel a wave of sadness or fear, or experience a flash of some forgotten disturbing event. Neither clinging to nor rejecting the disturbing experience, we let it pass. After the meditation period is over we can discern just what to do about the disturbing experience we got in touch with. In many instances, we may intuitively sense that nothing more needs be done. It was enough simply to feel the feelings and to be aware of the images that passed through us as we sat in meditation. Sometimes, however, we might experience the felt need to reflect on, journal, share with a trusted friend, or otherwise process and integrate into our conscious awareness the previously unprocessed material that we experienced in meditation.

In some instances the memories and emotions we tapped into in meditation may be of such magnitude as to warrant psychotherapy. This is especially so if the unprocessed material continues to leak out in symptoms of depression or anxiety, or to come out in other ways that indicate we may have come upon something within ourselves that we had best neither ignore nor try to deal with without help. As seekers of the contemplative way we should be more rather than less aware of our own unfinished business. We should be more, not less, responsible for working on those aspects of ourselves that cause us to continue to act out old patterns that compromise or do violence to the value and full potential of our own life and the lives of those around us.

Specific consideration must be given to those times in which we can become overwhelmed in meditation to the point of experiencing panic, terror, a foreboding sense of being in the presence of evil, a fear of losing one's mind, or profound, unbearable feelings of loss and isolation. Some people, many in fact, meditate for many years and never have these acutely disturbing experiences. But there are some who do have these experiences, and it is helpful to have some basic guidelines regarding just how to respond to them should they occur.

A basic response to extremely disturbing experiences that occur in meditation is to stop meditating immediately until one has had a chance to understand and process what has happened. As seekers of the contemplative way, we should be more, not less, committed to a position of nonviolence so that we never knowingly contribute to the traumatization of anyone, including ourselves. Upon reflection, the cause of the disturbing experience might be found to be the death of a loved one or some other painful loss one has not yet allowed oneself to grieve over. Or it may be some potentially disturbing event one is facing in the future that one has not yet allowed oneself to look at fully and honestly. When the cause of the disturbance is recognized and worked through, one can most often return to meditation without further incident.

These considerations of safety become all the more relevant with those who experience episodes of being lost in or flooded by painful emotions or destructive thinking. This would include those experiencing symptoms associated with bipolar disorder, major depression, anxiety with panic attacks, borderline personality disorder, dissociative disorders, or post traumatic stress associated with severe childhood abuse or more recent trauma. With proper guidance certain aspects of meditation can be a helpful adjunct to the treatment of these disorders. Generally speaking, however, the tendency of meditation to lower our defenses makes meditation potentially destructive to those who are having to work very hard just to find their defenses.

Realizing that it is not safe for one to meditate when one desires to do so is, understandably, a loss that needs to be faced and accepted. In being faced and accepted, however, one discovers one's self to be intimately learning things about the human heart. By humbly accepting and taking responsibility for oneself the way one is, by relying on spiritual reading and more structured forms of prayer and meditation, one lives out a particularly paradoxical way of being present, open, and awake to the inherent holiness of daily living. With time, as one reconstitutes and grows in ego strength, meditation may be fully available as one's primary contemplative practice. In fact, meditation may be all the more available, due to one's painfully acquired familiarity with and trust in the gentle light that inexplicably guided one through one's darkest moments.

The final season of body-grounded stillness we will consider here is that of a stillness so profound that no effort at all is required to sustain it. Some classical texts in the contemplative traditions speak of this state in terms of one's whole being becoming as still and serene as the surface of a lake across which not the slightest breeze passes. In entering into this state of effortless body-grounded serenity, we arrive at the resting place in which our self-transformation into God most clearly and decisively comes to pass. The following poetic image is intended to convey something of this wondrous state.

Imagine that you are on a large boat crossing a vast expanse of water. There are many people on the boat, all of whom are enjoying a party of some kind. In a moment of carelessness you fall off the back of the boat into the water. Everyone on the boat is having so much fun that no one sees that you have fallen overboard. Treading water, you yell and wave to no avail as the boat continues on its way, growing smaller and smaller, eventually disappearing into the distance. Realizing that you cannot tread water for very long, but that you can float for a long time, your strategy becomes that of floating until, hopefully, those on board will notice you are missing and, in doing so, will come back to rescue you. Now in order to float you have to relax, for if you tense up you sink. And so there you are, all alone in the vast expanse of water, floating, relaxing, floating, relaxing. How would you be relaxing out there? Knowing your life depended on it, you would be relaxing *very* seriously. You would be relaxing with all your heart. Each time fear arises, causing you to tense up, you renew the letting-go embodied in your life-saving relaxation. Tensing up, you relax, tensing up, you relax—a life saving dance in the midst of the sea!

Then a most extraordinary thing happens—floating there all alone, looking up into a boundless sky, it dawns on you that you are being sustained in a vast Presence that sustains you whether you live or die. While at one level it would be truly tragic to drown, to go under, to face the scary end, at yet another level, too big to think about, there arises a bliss beyond feeling. There is granted a body-grounded realization that even in going under you would remain sustained. You would remain safe in the undoing. Floating there, beyond the dualism of life and death, in a timeless moment beyond time, anchored invincibly in a boundless sky, you realize that in drowning you would become what you already are. You would become one with the primitive sea of unmanifested Presence your presence in the present moment is manifesting.

If, while floating in this wondrous awakening, you were suddenly to see the boat coming back to get you, you would no doubt experience a profound sense of relief and joy. In being pulled back on board, you might be overcome with emotion and weep that your life was saved. But deeper down within yourself you would know that you were being pulled back on board as one transformed in a great awakening. You would know that in some profound sense beyond the power of thought to grasp, beyond the ability of words to describe, you were saved out there in the midst of the sea, where, in an unto-death dance of choosing to relax, choosing to let go, you found a life beyond life and death.

As seekers of the contemplative way we have indeed fallen off the boat into the sea. At first the falling was isolated to our moments of spontaneous contemplative awakening in which we found ourselves momentarily sustained in a body-grounded awareness of the abyss-like nature of the concrete immediacy of the present moment. Each falling ends in being pulled back on board, which is to say, ends in our once again returning to our customary ways of experiencing the things to which we are accustomed. But little by little this pattern of falling and returning, falling and returning forms our character, making us someone whose daily living has become imbued with a quiet, inner desire to live in a more abiding awareness of the ever present depths. Our sitting still and straight in meditation is our free choice to leap into the sea. Or perhaps, more true to the experience, it is our free choice to ease ourselves over and over again into the fathomless sea of presence the present moment manifests. As we become seasoned in the self-transforming power of simply sitting, we become ever more habituated to a sustained state of body-grounded serenity. We become ever more habitually at home in a pure and simple awareness of the divinity of the present moment manifesting itself in and as all that arises, all that passes away.

Eyes Closed or Lowered Toward the Ground

The next suggested guideline for meditation practice is to sit with your eyes closed or lowered toward the ground. Some people find it is most natural and effective to close their eyes completely while they meditate. Others find that the Zen meditation method of sitting with the eyes slightly open, lowered toward the ground is most effective; they tend to be less prone to the sleepiness and imagery that tends to occur with their eyes completely closed. I will be referring here most often to sitting with one's eyes slightly open, lowered toward the ground, simply because this is what I am most used to in my own practice and, therefore, most able to explore poetically. As you settle into your meditation practice you will discover whether meditating with your eyes completely closed or slightly open is best for you, which is to say, which way most naturally embodies an interior stance of gazing directly into the abyss-like nature of the concrete immediacy of the present moment. If you find meditating with your eyes closed is best for you, the poetic imagery of this chapter may still be applicable to those times in which the visual dimension of your self-transformation expresses itself in moments of quietly gazing at works of art, or scenes of nature, the people you love, the objects in your own home.

Lowering our eyes in meditation is an act of incarnate faith in which the contemplative event of gazing deeply into the abyss-like nature of now comes to pass. I say comes to pass because at first lowering our eyes is experienced as being but a practical method facilitating present moment attentiveness: We begin our meditation. Sitting still, sitting straight, we see through our lowered eyes our hands in our lap, the design in the carpet or perhaps the cracks in the floorboards. We see the quality of light in which we see all these things: the intensity of midday sunlight, or perhaps the diffused light of a cloudy afternoon, or the faint light cast by a flickering candle. As we settle into the silent, childlike attentiveness of the practice, there is born in us the contemplative experience of gazing into the abyss-like nature of the concrete immediacy of the design in the carpet, the cracks in the floorboards, our hands in our lap, as transparently manifesting, in some overwhelmingly subtle manner, the unmanifested Presence we call God. Sitting thus, gazing into this depth of divinity the present moment manifests, we practice our practice, so that, little by little, this contemplative stance of quietly beholding the divinity of the present moment might find its way into our daily awareness of our daily living.

In order to better understand and appreciate the gazing aspect of our meditation practice, we can step back to explore the gazing aspect of our moments of spontaneous contemplative experience, noting how they contain both focused and unfocused aspects, which spontaneously arise together and play about one another as the contemplative experience unfolds. Sometimes this interplay begins with the focused aspect spontaneously arising as we become so completely absorbed in one thing that all else momentarily vanishes. The unfocused aspect then comes into play as all that has vanished re-appears as contemplatively realized through the aperture of the one thing in which we are completely absorbed. We turn to see a flock of birds descending or children at play. Suddenly, the whole universe falls away in a moment of complete absorption in these birds descending, these children at play. As if pressing our face up against and peering through the aperture of their divinity, we see the divinity of all birds, of all children, of all things, of all that is and is not, as evidenced by our coming away from the experience with a heightened appreciation of birds, of children, of all things.

The interplay begins the other way around, in those times when contemplative experience first arises as our gazing upon the totality of the whole scene. With the sky above us, the earth beneath our feet, we are awakened to an all encompassing totality[2] in which a single thing, a bird, a child, suddenly stands out with unprecedented clarity.

The focused and unfocused aspects of contemplative beholding spontaneously play about one another of their own accord, forming together the visual realization of the totality-manifested-in-each-thing, each-thing-manifesting-the-totality nature of the contemplatively realized, real world.

You are walking along the beach, being present to the totality of the experience of simply being at the primordial meeting place of land and sea, when a shell at your feet catches your eye. Stopping, you stoop down, pick it up, and holding it the palm of your hand, all else falls away as you become, for one sustained moment, utterly absorbed in the shell's delicate beauty. Then, you look up to see the countless shells stretched out before you, one with the whole scene of sky, shoreline, birds, the one wave that is in this precise instant washing up over your bare feet. Then, looking down, you see once again the shell in your hand, being the one shell that it alone uniquely is in this just-the-way-it-is, present-moment totality. So it is that the now focused, now unfocused aspects of awareness, work together, like a great bellows of the eyes, fanning the flames of enlightenment, deepening the contemplative awareness of the totality-in-each-thing, each-thing-in-the-totality nature of reality.

The meditation practice of sitting still and straight with our eyes lowered toward the ground is a method of cultivating the sustained awareness of the playful interplay of the focused and unfocused awareness of the one in all, all in one nature of the contemplatively realized, real world. Sitting still and straight in an ever deepening body-grounded wakefulness, you gaze through your lowered eyes into the concrete immediacy of the cracks in the floorboards, the design in the carpet. Your eyes naturally focus on a single aspect of the totality, perhaps a particular section of a single crack in the flooring that is a bit wider or more narrow than the others or perhaps on how the flooring shines in the sunlight or perhaps, how the carpet's edging is frayed in one particular place. But you do not cling to this focused awareness; rather you let it pass of its own accord as you remain established in the more global sense of the totality of all that is seen. But in becoming once again aware of a more global awareness of all that is seen, you do not cling to this more global awareness. You do not choose this more global awareness over the beholding of the concrete immediacy of each detail of each thing that is gazed upon.

As we give ourselves over to this gazing there rises up out of the cracks in the floorboard, the designs in the carpet, the concreteness of all that is seen, an intimate vision of the all-in-one, one-in-all unitive nature of reality. Contemplative wisdom is born of this seeing, a wisdom that realizes that to see clearly the concrete details of the world around us is good, for this is to be an astute observer of our surrounding. But to see the concrete details of all that appears without intuitively seeing the all encompassing totality the details manifest is not to see the true interconnected nature of all that we see. Likewise, to seek God or to seek enlightenment or holiness is good, for this is to seek our ultimate fulfillment. But to seek divine fulfillment as wholly other than and beyond the concrete immediacy of the present moment is to be blind to the transcendence of God's immanence, which is to say blind to the way our divine fulfillment is already at hand in and as the situation at hand.

Contemplative gazing is the visual expression of the self-transforming journey in which we are set free from the twofold ignorance of seeing things as opaque to God as we simultaneously see God to be dualistically other than the concrete immediacy of things. In the contemplative gaze the concrete immediacy of the present moment is seen to be the manifestation of the unmanifested mystery of God, as God is simultaneously seen to be the infinity of the mystery the present moment manifests.

We are, of course, in no way excluded from the contemplatively realized all-in-one, one-in-all nature of the real world. How could we be excluded from the unitive nature of reality when, in the moment of our contemplative awakening we are the one in whom this all-in-one, one-in-all nature of reality is realized? Meditation is not a spectator sport in which we stand back and observe, in objective fashion, a unity from which we ourselves are dualistically excluded. To the contrary, in meditation we open ourselves to the self-transforming awareness of our oneness with the mystery we seek manifesting itself in and as our experience of it. The phrase, "our experience of *it*" belies the inadequacy of words to express the unitive mystery contemplative experiences realizes. To the extent this unitive awareness is realized, there is no "it" to it. That is to say, there is no mystery other than ourselves being realized. Nor is there a self realizing a mystery other than itself. The clearer and deeper the contemplative experience becomes, the more clearly our very subjectivity is realized to be itself a manifestation of the mystery we seek, manifesting itself in and as our very subjectivity. Contemplative gazing is the visual expression of this unitive experience, in which we do not simply see the divinity of all that we see, but what is more come to realize the divinity of our seeing all that we see.

Jesus said, "You have eyes to see and do not see." As read in the context of contemplative self-transformation, Jesus' words illuminate the fact that the *way we see* the present moment is the visual expression of the way we tend to *be* in the present moment. To say that we have eyes to see and yet do not see, is to express in visual terms the plight of our ignorance in which we go about as manifestations of the divine seeking union with the divine. The entire path of self-transformation can be articulated in these visual terms in saying that we move along the path of our self-transformation in dying to egocentric modes of seeing that blind us to the divinity of the life we are living. In this dying process we simultaneously grow into a more contemplative mode of seeing in which the divinity of the life we are living is realized.

We can recognize several different modes of seeing, each exhibiting a point on the continuum moving from egocentric to contemplative modes of consciousness. The wide eyed boldness of the hostile stare, for example, is decidedly distinct from the contemplative gaze. We cannot stare our way into the depths. For in the steely harshness of the intrusive stare the concrete immediacy of the present remains opaque to us. We instinctively become guarded the instant we sense someone is staring at us in a manner suggesting a less than loving intent. So, too, the divinity of the present moment seems to close itself off from our intrusive stare, as if sensing an attempted forced entry into its depths.

Similarly, gawking has about it an egocentric tonality that is quite distinct from the contemplative gaze. Gawking is a crass form of egocentric seeing limited to a momentary amazement at some external characteristic that stands out to us simply because what we are seeing is, in some startling manner, outside the range of what we are accustomed to seeing. A man seven feet tall walking into a restaurant is gawked at, as is the singer with a fifty-inch bust-line and twenty-inch waist who has just walked out on stage to belt out her song. Both momentarily capture our attention, even as they know full well they remain essentially unseen by us as we look upon them.

If, in the exercise of our religious imagination, we were to choose whether staring or gazing is most continuous with the way the blessed see God in paradise, most of us would, most likely, intuitively choose gazing.

It seems counter-intuitive to think of the blessed in paradise staring at God with all the intrusive harshness that staring implies. Similarly, if we were to choose whether gawking or gazing is most continuous with the way the blessed see God in paradise, most of us would, most likely, choose gazing. It seems counter-intuitive to think that in paradise you can tell the newcomers, those who have been in heaven for only a few centuries or so, because they are still gawking at God like open-mouthed tourists! Intuitively we can sense the continuity of gazing with our eternal destiny in that gazing is that mode of intimate, non-intrusive seeing that attains to the living essence of that which is gazed upon. Gazing is that mode of intimate seeing in which all otherness is transcended as an ineffable communion wordlessly realized. In gazing the eyes are allowed to open, free of the egocentric intrusions of intention in which we seek to lay our eyes on any particular thing to meet any particular need. In the contemplative gaze we simply behold all that is simply seen, allowing our eyes to lead the way into a contemplative realization the present moment's simply given divinity.

A moment of contemplative gazing is a way of seeing that sets us free, transforming our customary more egocentric ways of being in the present moment. This metamorphosis begins anew with each new moment of spontaneous contemplative experience in which we find ourselves being the way we deep down really are, one with the way the present moment deep down really is. The metamorphosis born of moments of spontaneous experience continues in the form of the painful void that accompanies the passing of such moments. As the moment of spontaneous contemplative awakening passes and we return to our customary way of being in the present moment, we can see, by way of comparison to the contemplative moment just experienced, just how blind we tend to be to the ever present divinity of the life we are living. But instead of stopping short at the pain arising from seeing how blind we tend to be of the divinity of our daily living, we can instead choose to gaze into this blindness as a way of seeing ever more clearly how little we see. And as we yield to this visual expression of our enlightened ignorance, we can yield as well to the holy discontent that impels us to sit in meditation with wholehearted "Lord-that-I-might-see" sincerity.

Our understanding and appreciation of this self-transforming process of learning to see by way of gazing into our inability to see can perhaps be enhanced by observing its appearance in the literal sense in which someone discovers he or she has just lost, or is in the process of losing, their eyesight. Imagine a man who loses his eyesight in a tragic accident. At first he thrashes about in a tumult of mixed emotions. But, then, in the midst of his suffering, there emerges the graced event of an inner stillness and repose in which he gazes deeply into the darkness that has become his home. At the level of ego, his loss remains a truly tragic event that calls for massive adjustment at a number of different levels. But interiorly, at the level that determines the fundamental tonality of his presence in the world, he stands the chance of discovering, in a most intimate fashion, what so often proves to be true: Loss leaves an empty space, a gaping hole in the should-be, always-thought-it-would-be world in which the ego tries so hard to live. It is into this empty space, occasioned by the loss his eyesight, that he now gazes, interiorly being transformed in accepting all that he sees. The transformation undergone by such a person accounts for the simple truth that there are those who are blind who, with respect to what matters most, see quite clearly. And, inversely, there are those of us with perfect or near perfect eyesight who, with respect to what matters most, do not see so well.

This same theme can be expanded to blindness at the psychological level when a person is seriously committed to working through long term, deep seated disturbances, such at those related to alcoholism, bipolar disorder, or the long term effects of severe childhood trauma. There are, of course, the obvious benefits gained in the recovery process in terms of heightened levels of functioning. There is, as well, the spiritual metamorphosis arising from gazing long and hard, in a compassionate, honest, and vulnerable manner into one's brokenness. In so doing one has the chance of discovering first hand the stuff of which the heart is made. In a no nonsense, down-to-earth kind of a way, one hits bottom. In so doing one discovers that the bottom gives way to a yet deeper depth in which is granted an intimate experience of the divinity of ourselves as invincibly lovable and whole in all our fragmentation.

The whole of the spiritual life moves in accordance with the primitive rhythms of this paradoxical vision of life and reality in which we come to discover that it is a painful privilege to live in the awareness of our unawareness. Each new moment of spontaneous contemplative experience comes like a lightening flash in the night, fleetingly disclosing the divinity of the present moment. The darkness that quickly returns is the empty space, the gaping hole in the should-be, always-thought-it-would-be world of divinity in which the child self born of God tries so hard to live. But by learning to gaze deeply into our daily blindness to the divinity of our daily living, we are not humiliated but humbled. And in being humbled we are made wise by learning to see and accept ourselves as we really are. The more we see how little we see, the more we are able to see, in an interior, intimate manner, the mystery that we, in our better seeing days, were unable to see. The more we see how little we see, the more we see, in a graced manner we cannot explain, the overflowing goodness that sustains and wholly permeates us as precious and whole in all our wayward ways.

In our willingness to live like this, our meditation practice of lowering our eyes toward the ground becomes a faith-act that embodies our day-by-day desire to see the divinity our daily life embodies. And so we sit, gazing down at a floor that, more often than not, remains stubbornly opaque to our gaze. We sit, gazing downward, remaining as powerless as ever to see the divinity we know, by way of our own past moments of contemplative experience, to be always before our eyes. The limited field of vision created by lowering our eyes toward the ground embodies the limited field of vision in which we acknowledge ourselves to be living. Sitting thus, in this humble acceptance of ourselves in our blindness, our lowered eyes become the narrow gate through which we pass into the deeper place.

Sitting thus, gazing into this depth, our eyes tell the story of our life up till now as one who, having fleetingly glimpsed the divinity of now, seeks to live day by day in the intimate vision of the divinity of now's ceaseless flow. We cannot tell this story in words, our hearts break when we try. Words fail us in their linear limits, sequentially stretching out in many ideas what happens all at once in an immediacy before thought begins. And so we sit, our story told, our identity revealed in this wordless gazing into the depths of the moment in which we sit. Sitting thus, we gaze directly into "the uncertain world of birth and death."[3] Sitting thus, we gaze directly into the face of God manifested in and as the abyss-like nature of the concrete immediacy of the one unending present moment in which our lives unfold. Sitting thus, our gaze incarnates the truth of Meister Eckhart's utterance, "the eye in which I see God is the same eye in which God sees me."[4]

Hands in a Comfortable or Meaningful Position

When we sit in meditation we place our hands in a comfortable or meaningful position in our lap. You may find it most natural simply to place your open hands, palm downward or upward, on each thigh. Or you may find it most natural to sit with your hands, palms up, joined together, with one hand gently resting on top of the other.

You may place your hands in a particular position simply because it is the one that feels most natural to you. Or you may find yourself holding your hands in a certain position because of an interiorly sensed symbolic meaning that particular position has for you. For example, you may find that sitting with your palms turned upward on each thigh may symbolize an attitude of receptive openness. Or your upturned hands, one resting gently in the other, may symbolize an empty cup you are waiting for God to fill. You may be inclined to hold your hands in yet some other position that may hold for you its own particular meaning. I have seen people sitting in meditation with their hands resting one each thigh, palms upward, with the thumb and the tip of the first finger joined together. I have seen others sitting with their palms joined together at the level of their heart, their fingers pointing upward in a position of prayer.

A hand position may also be meaningful in the context of following the prescribed hand positions of a particular Buddhist or Hindu yoga school of meditation. In attempting to learn any of these methods of meditation, you will, of course, want to consult books written by qualified teachers in these traditions. Preferable to this, of course, is finding a qualified teacher in these traditions, who can instruct you in all aspects of that tradition's meditation practices, including the positions in which the hands are traditionally held. I personally have become accustomed to the Zen tradition of resting one hand in the other, palms upward, then forming a circle by gently bringing one's thumbs together until the tips of the thumbs barely touch.

What matters, of course, is not the specific position in which we hold our hands, but that we allow the stillness of our hands to embody our whole hearted commitment to a work not made with human hands, a work not composed of compound things. This work is that of yielding to the graced event of our ongoing contemplative self-transformation in which we are intimately awakened to the divinity of who we simply are, one with the sheer immediacy of all the present moment simply is.

Slow, Deep, Natural Breathing

Slow, deep, natural breathing is another fundamental aspect of meditation practice. Sitting still and straight, our eyes closed or lowered toward ground, we establish ourselves in a childlike awareness of each breath. Breathing out we are quietly aware of breathing out. Breathing in we are quietly aware of breathing in. In this way, our awareness becomes one with the primitive rhythms of our breathing, one with the simply given nature of now's ceaseless flow in which our life is rooted.

There are several different methods of breath awareness in Zen meditation that anyone can incorporate into meditation practice. These methods include sitting straight, breathing slowly and deeply, with one's abdomen, rather than one's chest, moving in and out as one breathes. Awareness of the breath can be focused on the subtle sensation of air that can be felt at your nostrils and upper lip as you breathe with your mouth closed. Another method is to let your awareness descend and settle into your abdomen moving in and out with each breath. Some Zen sources suggest fostering breath awareness by counting each breath up to ten, going back to one if you lose count. Other sources suggest focusing full attention on each breath without counting. In time and with practice you will settle in to the method of breath awareness that is best for you, which is to say, the method that most effectively awakens you to the divinity of life each breath manifests.

When we first sit to meditate breath awareness serves as an anchoring place in present moment attentiveness. Each and every time we drift off into this or that, we bring ourselves back to the present moment by focusing full attention on the breath. As our practice deepens, our ego merges with the flow of the breath, becoming indistinguishable from the breath itself. It is something like a dancer, who can use dancing as a way of keeping in shape. This is like sitting in ego consciousness using the breath as a tool or means of improving one's powers of concentration. Or the dancer can become aware of her dancing for its own sake, consciously noticing how she could improve this or that aspect of it. This is like sitting in meditation intent on improving our methods of breath awareness. Or the dancer can so give herself over to the dance as to become indistinguishable from it. In the ecstasy of this oneness she, and all who look upon her, realize something of what heaven is like. This is like sitting in meditation so merged with the simply given miracle of each breath as to know something of the miraculous ways of God giving herself to us in and as this breath . . . this breath . . . this breath. As our practice deepens by way of this communion with our breathing, we come to discover that breath awareness is more than enough to carry us all the way home. As Eido T. Shimano, a Zen master in New York City, expressed it, "In meditation right effort is full attention on the breath. Right attitude is forgetting everything else."[5]

When we sit in meditation, focusing full attention on the breath, we should do so as a student on the first day of class sits in awe before a world renowned teacher of the contemplative way. Sitting still and straight in body-grounded attentiveness, we learn, breath by breath, the lessons this great teacher has to offer. One of these lessons is that of learning to enter into the flow of the unity that reigns within and without.

Slow, deep, natural breathing awakens us to the unity that reigns within by bringing to light and dissolving the obstacles to it. Eido Roshi once said in a conference at the Naropa Institute, "the devil is a tight diaphragm." We go through life, cut in half, with a ligature about our middle, which crimps off our experience of all the unacknowledged and disavowed aspects of ourselves. When we first sit in meditation we sit with this ligature about our middle, afraid to be as broken and whole, as weak and strong, as ephemeral and invincible, as fleeting and eternal, as human and divine as we really are. Slow, deep, natural breathing invites a gentle dissolution of the ligature, a slow dissolving of the barriers, a melting of all restraints. You might imagine that with each inhalation you are breathing down into the whole of yourself, down through the soles of your feet, down through all that you are in a "Here I am, Lord," stance of interior openness. You might imagine that each exhalation is coming up through the soles of your feet, up through all that you are. So that back and forth, up and down, your breathing creates pathways of openness to the unity that reigns within.

The existential psychologist Rollo May observed that while repressed sexuality was the neurosis of Freud's age, it is hardly the neurosis of our age. The neurosis of our age, May suggests, is the fear of being all that we are. Afraid of being all that we are, we pretend to be less than we are. But because, at some level, we know we are pretending, we experience anxiety that our charade will be discovered and we will have to stand up and become all that we really are and are called to be. Being all that we are entails, as its starting point, opening ourselves to all that we are. Breath awareness embodies and brings about this openness, not by force, but by simply loosening the constraints. Loosening the constraints, breath by breath, gives rise to an unencumbered openness, in which a more unitive and all encompassing sense of a self that is one with God begins to emerge.

Sitting still and straight in wholehearted attentiveness to each breath also invites an awareness of one's essential unity with all that lies outside oneself. If, at the count of ten, all the air were to be instantaneously removed from the room in which you are now sitting, there would be no inhalation for you at the count of eleven. Such is your breath by breath radical dependency on the air that surrounds you. And the air that surrounds you and sustains you, surrounds and sustains me as I sit here writing these words that you are now reading, just as it surrounds and sustains all who live. Sitting in body-grounded awareness of each breath, we enter into a body-grounded awareness of the unitive life each breath embodies and sustains. Grounded in this awareness, we come to realize, in a most intimate fashion, what we have long known in a factual, so-what, kind of way; namely, that we do not and cannot exist without the universe that sustains us and of which we are a part. We do not and cannot exist apart from others, one with us in our breath by breath communal dependency on the earth that sustains us all.

As the meditative state deepens and expands we come to an intimate realization that the unity that reigns within and without constitutes one single unity. Each exhalation is the world within flowing outward. Each inhalation is the outer world flowing inward. Back and forth, in and out, the freely flowing inter-penetration of the inner and outer worlds weaves the seamless garment of the intuitively realized real world. In this wondrous awakening the distinction between inside and outside, between all that I am and all that is other than who I am, remains even as it is transcended in the realization of a unity that wholly permeates and embraces as one, all that is without, all that is within.

Another lesson learned in breath awareness is the lesson of the neglected essential. I used to keep a small poster on my desk that read, "Things to do today: inhale, exhale, inhale, exhale, inhale, exhale." Breathing is not on the day's to-do list because breathing is not something we have to think about doing. The breath flows of its own accord as the neglected essential without which all the important items on the to-do list could never be done.

Imagine a man sitting in deep meditation, seeking perfect union with God, who has a massive heart attack and dies. His search for God met with sudden unplanned success! Such is the thread that flows from God, the sovereignty of our fragility. Sitting in bare attention of the breath, we sit given over to this sovereign fragility. At birth, the first breath; at death, the last; and in between the unbroken thread of the breath by breath grace of the simply given life we are living. This is the homecoming wisdom to which breath awareness awakens us.

What if our breathing or our beating heart, or for that matter all our bodily movements, required a continually repeated conscious choice. What if our daily life was, at this radical, fundamental level, up to us to maintain. What if, for our heart to keep beating, we had to remember to continue the interior, conscious intention: beat, beat; to continue breathing we had to remember to continue intending to now inhale, now exhale; to walk we had to consciously say to our left leg, then to our right leg: move, move. And what if, such being the case, we were absent minded! The anxiety of facing the consequences of a forgotten breath or heartbeat would be overwhelming. Fortunately, such is not the case. We are carried along in a flow of the essential life, without which all the important choices, profound conclusions, and important projects would not, could not, occur. Breath awareness teaches us to be less neglectful of the moment by moment, simply given life that we live.

Being less neglectful of the essential, more humbly grounded in it, everything we do and say begins to flow more directly from this simply given ground. In sweeping a floor, for example, we might find ourselves identifying not so much with getting it finished, but rather with the intimate realization of how this simple act embodies and expresses the neglected essential of being real and alive in this moment in this place, engaged in this act of sweeping this floor. The more habitual and natural this kind of awareness of daily events becomes, the more confident and grateful we can be that we are on the path that leads to a more contemplative way of life in the midst of the circumstances in which we find ourselves.

Finally, we can consider how breath awareness teaches us the lessons of receiving, of letting go, and of the equality of receiving and letting go. Each inhalation *is* an act of receiving the simply given nature of life itself. The Christian mystic Meister Eckhart said, "For God to be is to give being. For us, to be is to receive being."[6] Our very being is an act of receiving the act of being that God infinitely is. Each inhalation embodies this receiving perfectly. A friend of mine shared with me that soon after his wife came home from the hospital after the birth of their first child, she went out alone for a short shopping trip, leaving him alone for the first time with his infant daughter. He said that he lay on the sofa, putting his sleeping infant daughter on his chest, with her mouth near his ear. Lying there motionless in complete silence, listening to the sheer miracle of her breath, he became filled with a sense of amazement and gratitude for the miracle of her newly emerging life. When we sit in meditation we listen to our breathing in this same manner. Sitting still and straight in meditation, leaning into each inhalation with such childlike abandon as to wholly lose our balance in the mystery of receiving the miracle of our simply given life, we are awakened to God giving herself to us, in and as the inhalation that is being received. Wholly attentive to our simply given life we sit open to the realization that our very presence is an act of receiving the very Presence that God infinitely is.

Just as each inhalation is the body-grounded act of receiving, so too with each exhalation our body teaches us the way of letting go of all that hinders our self-transformation into God. Perhaps each contemplative practice, including meditation, is as much as anything else, a way of letting go of all that hinders our becoming ever more aware of and transparently obedient to who we eternally are in the immediacy of the present moment.

The healing process of facing and working through psychological symptoms and difficulties can be seen as having a contemplative dimension in which one's healing consists of letting go of confining, destructive, and ultimately illusory ways of experiencing and expressing oneself. Harry Stack Sullivan, most known for his work in interpersonal psychology, expressed this letting go aspect of psychological healing in observing that on the surface it appears that the therapist and client are alone in the therapist's office. But, observes Sullivan, in a more interior sense it is not so, for sitting there on the sofa next to the client is the client's mother or father, husband or wife, employer or pastor, son or daughter. It is, in fact, quite crowded on that sofa. So much so that there is barely room there for the client, which probably has a great deal to do with why the client is in therapy!

A similar point can be made of our meditation practice. It may appear, on the surface, that we are alone in our chair or on our cushion as we meditate. But, in a more interior sense, it is not so. For there within us are all the internalized images of our past encounters with our father or mother, brother or sister, schoolmate, enemy, or lover. As we sit in meditation, surrendering to and moving with the flow of each exhalation, we learn to let go of clinging to and rejecting all that lies within.

Here is a path of self-transformation so immediately present as to bewilder, from the start, the ego's efforts to find it. The path consists of yielding to each exhalation to the point of allowing the mystery of letting go to dispossess us of all traces of possessiveness. Each exhalation tutors our heart in this allowing, this letting go, in which we find ourselves to be as open and free as we deep down really are and are called to be.

As we sit still and straight, entering with each inhalation into the lessons of receiving, and with each exhalation into the lessons of letting go, we learn as well the lesson of the equality of receiving and letting go, the equality of gain and loss, of all forms of birth and death. The breath embodies the dynamic reciprocity of gain and loss, of all forms of birth and death. To see how this is so we have but to imagine trying to sit in meditation for twenty minutes only exhaling. This is not advised. Nor is it possible, for each exhalation is possible only by virtue of having inhaled. Attempting to meditate for twenty minutes only inhaling, would be equally impossible, for each inhalation is possible only be virtue of the exhalation that precedes it. All life is like this.

We all share in common the inevitability of our eventual diminishment and death. But had we never been born, we would not be facing the inevitability of death. The French painter Rouault painted a nude woman in her final months of pregnancy. She is looking downward, as if lost in a moment of pensive silence. The caption at the bottom of painting reads, "Everyone must die. Even the one who has not yet been born must die." In the kind of pensive moment we rarely allow ourselves, the mother-to-be is pondering the inevitability of death inscribed into the very origins of her own life, the life of her unborn child, the life of all living things.

But if life, from its first moments onward is full of death, death from its first moments onward is full of life. Jesus said that "unless the grain of wheat fall into the ground and die it remains alone. But if it dies it brings forth fruit a hundred fold" (Jn 12:24). Our faith tells us that he was referring at once to himself and to us in our share in the mystery of his resurrection. Our contemplative pondering of the imagery of wheat dying and being born a hundredfold helps us to step into the vision of Jesus, seeing the mystery of death and resurrection in the cyclic mystery of our bodily being. Sitting in bare attention to each inhalation giving way to each exhalation giving way to each inhalation, we experience directly that our bodily being is inexorably woven into the cosmic dance of all of life, perpetually arising, perpetually falling away.

Our contemplative pondering of our life up till now discloses our own unique story of the equality of birth and death. Looking back to see how we became who we thus far have come to be, we see a pattern of an ongoing self-metamorphosis in which who we presently are is perpetually passing away. The passing away perpetually gives rise to the emergence of what we have never before been, which in turn ripens and dies, creating the fertile ground in which the perpetual impermanence of life continues to emerge.

Sitting in bare attention to each inhalation giving way to each exhalation giving way to each inhalation, we are intimately awakened to the primordial dance of gain unto loss, loss unto gain that flows through all of life, including our own. This primordial dance is the essential nature of the one unending present moment in which we sit and in which our lives unfold. Sitting still and straight, given over to the circularity of receiving and letting go that breathing embodies, we realize we cannot make the moment last. For it is the nature of the moment not to last as it yields to what we call the future, and in so doing becomes what we call the past. And we see that this not lasting quality of the present moment is the way the present moment always is. And

in seeing this, we see the permanence of impermanence. We see the way not lasting lasts in experiencing
the not lasting quality of now to be the very nothing-
ness out of which the newness of the present moment
ceaselessly arises. Our faith calls the abyss-like ground of
this mystery God—the infinity of the never lasting now
that forever lasts.

Present, Open, and Awake, Neither Clinging to nor Rejecting Anything

When we meditate we are to sit in a sustained contemplative stance of being present, open, and awake,
neither clinging to nor rejecting anything. This directive applies from the very first moment we sit, in that
from the very first moment we hear sounds—a heater or
fan running, a radio playing in another room, a car driving past. We become aware of bodily sensations; our
knee starts to hurt, tension begins to build between our
shoulders, or perhaps there is a pervasive sense of bodily contentment. We become aware of emotions; a wave
of sadness, fear, or happiness. Images appear before the
mind's eye: disturbing images, sexual images, bizarre
images, beautiful images, religious images. There are
thoughts, the ongoing flow of all kinds of thoughts.
With regard to all these matters of the mind, the guiding principle is to remain present, open, and awake, neither clinging to nor rejecting anything.

Numerous passages could be cited in the classical
texts of the contemplative traditions of the world's great
religions which encourage the cultivation of a contemplative awareness that transcends our customary
reliance on thought and feeling. For example, the
anonymous author of the fourteenth century Christian
classic *The Cloud of Unknowing* offers practical guidelines
in the practice of contemplative prayer, which consists
essentially of establishing oneself in a sustained stance
of loving desire for God alone. In this stance of love

alone, the author urges, "Do all in your power to forget everything else, keeping your thoughts and desires free from involvement with any of God's creatures or their affairs whether in general or in particular." The author makes clear that sustaining this loving awareness is not easy at first. For in learning to wean yourself from your customary reliance on thought, "You will seem to know nothing and to feel nothing except a naked intent toward God in the depths of your being." But, he urges, "Learn to be at home in this darkness. . . . For, if in this life, you hope to feel and see God as he is in himself it must be within this darkness. . . ."[7]

The sixteenth century Spanish mystic Saint John of the Cross gives three signs by which a person can discern that he or she is being led by God beyond discursive meditation, with its reliance on thought and feeling, to contemplation. John states that the surest of these three signs is that "a person likes to remain alone in loving awareness of God, without particular considerations in interior peace, quiet and repose. . . . Such a one likes to remain only in the general loving awareness and knowledge—without any particular knowledge or understanding." He goes on to say concerning this state of general loving awareness that "I am not affirming the imagination will cease to come and go (even in the deep recollection it usually wanders freely), but that the person is disinclined to fix it purposely upon extraneous things."[8] One simply sits, given over to a general loving awareness in which one neither clings to nor rejects any memory, thought, or emotion that may arise and pass through one's awareness as one simply sits.

Similar passages can be found in the classical sources of Buddhist contemplative wisdom. The ninth century Chinese Zen master Huang Po wrote "not till you abandon all thoughts of seeking for something, not till your mind is motionless as wood or stone, will you be on the right road to the Gate. The approach to it is called the Gateway of the Stillness beyond all activities."[9] The thirteenth century Japanese Zen master Eihei Dogen, giving instructions in the fundamentals of meditation practice, wrote, "Sit solidly in *samadhi* (a serene, settled state of mind) and think not-thinking. How do you think not-thinking? Nonthinking."[10] That is, simply sit, abandoning all reliance on conceptual information and instruction. Just sit serenely, with all your heart, awake to but neither clinging to nor rejecting the thoughts that come and go as you sit. And the Zen Master Sengstan stated, "The great way is not difficult for those who have no preferences. . . . To set up what you like against what you dislike is the disease of the mind."[11]

Numerous other texts could be cited in both Christian and Buddhist sources. To these texts numerous others could be added from the Hasidic and *kabbalah* traditions of Judaism, the Sufi tradition of Islam, the yoga traditions of Hinduism, Taoist and other traditions, all giving witness to a universal pattern of offering guidance and encouragement in cultivating a contemplative awareness transcending the confines of thought and feeling.

The hidden origins of the universal wisdom of the contemplative traditions of the world's religions mysteriously arises in each of us in our moments of spontaneous contemplative experience. In these moments we suddenly transcend our customary reliance on thought and feeling in sensing directly the awe evoking mystery manifested in children at play or a flock of birds descending. The path marked out by the primitive wisdom of the contemplative traditions appears beneath our own feet as we find ourselves seeking ways to establish ourselves in a more daily, abiding awareness of the depths so fleetingly glimpsed in our moments of spontaneous experience. And the communal wisdom of the contemplative traditions as to how to go about realizing a more habitual, daily awareness of the divinity of daily living is embodied in our sitting still and straight, given over to the simple, childlike intention of being present, open and awake neither clinging to nor rejecting anything. To adapt a lovely phrase found in the Buddhist work, *The Blue Cliff Record*,[12] when we sit in meditation, present, open, and awake, neither clinging to nor rejecting anything, the hairs of our eyebrows are entangled with the eyebrows of the saints and mystics down through the ages. Sitting, present, open, and awake, the mystical body of all contemplative seekers, one with God, lives on in and as our awakened bodily presence in the present moment.

Actually, we have been exploring contemplative mindfulness from the onset of these reflections on meditation practice. We have been exploring how sitting still with all one's heart awakens the mind of stillness, one with the divinity of now's ceaseless flow. Sitting straight with all one's heart sustains the descent into the mind that sees and accepts all that lies within. Sitting in meditation, closing or lowering our eyes in a "Lord, that I might see" (Mk 10:51) stance of contemplative attentiveness awakens the mind that gazes directly into "the uncertain world of birth and death."[13] Sitting with our hands in a comfortable or meaningful position in our lap embodies the mindfulness born of surrendering ourselves over to the mystery not made with human hands. Slow, deep, natural breathing awakens the mind that knows the equality of birth and death. But now we focus our attention specifically on what we tend to think of as our mind, which is to say on our awareness of the sensations, thoughts, emotions, and memories that are experienced in meditation. With respect to all these matters of the mind, the directive is to be present, open, and awake, neither clinging to nor rejecting anything. Let us see how this directive is carried out first with respect to the thoughts that occur during meditation.

A distinction can be made between two different ways of experiencing the thoughts that arise in meditation. There are those thoughts that are experienced as passing through the field of awareness continuous with our overall experience of all that we are experiencing. And there are those thoughts that are experienced as carrying us away from the concrete immediacy of our body-grounded wakefulness in the present moment.

In the first of these two ways of experiencing the thoughts that arise in meditation, we sit still and straight, with slow deep natural breathing, our eyes closed or lowered toward the ground. As we sit we become aware of a thought, then another, then another passing through our field of awareness, continuous with our awareness of all that we are experiencing. In meditation there is no attempt to reject this contextual awareness of thoughts. Indeed, any attempt to do so is a potential intrusion of the ego into the nature of the moment just the way it is. For just as God creates the body to breathe, God creates the mind to think. Even in our sleep, the mind continues its incessant activity in the form of dreams. Awake or asleep, the flow of the mind's activity has a certain interminable quality, expressive of the endless nature of mind.

Just as the floor, the furnishings, and other details of the room in which we sit in meditation manifests the exteriority of the concrete immediacy of the present moment, so too, the thought that is presently passing through our field of awareness manifests the interiority of the concrete immediacy of the present moment. We sit in meditation not to reject, rearrange, or otherwise impose our will on the concrete immediacy of the present moment, but to recognize the simply given, utterly unfathomable nature of all that lies within, of all that lies without. We sit in meditation not to banish thought, but to learn to recognize and reverence the divinity of thought, the divinity of all that is and is not.

As we sit in meditation, we can see how each thought, if simply observed, without being clung to or rejected, simply arises, endures, and passes away. Just like the day or night in which you are meditating is arising, enduring, and passing away; just like your whole life is arising, enduring, and passing away; just like the whole universe is arising, enduring, and passing away; so, too, the thought you are now experiencing is arising, enduring, and passing away. The flow of thoughts that we experience in meditation is then not an adversary to be conquered, but rather the direct revelation of the eternal mystery of God, manifested in and as the eternal impermanence of thought, one with the eternal impermanence of all manifested reality. We are sitting in meditation not to abolish thought, but rather to gaze deeply into the eternal mystery the impermanence of thought manifests.

The focused and unfocused aspects of gazing which we explored earlier, are the visual expressions of a more general interior stance of contemplative mindfulness in both its focused and unfocused aspects. We sit, present, open, and awake to the concrete immediacy of the present moment. In hearing a car drive by outside, we simply hear the car driving by as playing its own part in the concrete immediacy of the present moment. We do not focus on the sound to the exclusion of the global, whole-hearted attentiveness to all that is experienced. Nor do we try to not hear the sound as if it were an intrusion into a sequestered silence. So too, with each thought that arises in meditation and with all else that makes up the concrete immediacy of the moment. Neither clinging to nor rejecting all that arises, endures, and passes away, we enter ever deeper into a childlike attentiveness of the fathomless depths of divinity the present moment manifests.

Lovers instinctively seek out places conducive to experiencing and sharing their love. In eating together, for example, they might choose a quiet, candle lit restaurant, conducive to the graced event in which eating together awakens and deepens their shared experience of being together. In having found such a setting, they are open to all they experience in it. They do not try to block out their awareness of the design in the china or the people sitting around them. But neither do they allow these things to distract them from the unitive event of their communal sharing. Rather, all they experience about them is experienced in the contextual wholeness of the love event of their being together.

Similarly, we instinctively seek out quiet places conducive to meditation—a church, a secluded place in the midst of nature, a quiet area of our own home. When we arrive at our chosen place of meditation and begin to meditate we do not block out our awareness of our surroundings. Rather, we settle in to an ever deeper realization of the divinity of the simply given nature of ourselves, one with our surroundings, one with all that is and is not. We settle into a childlike awareness in which all that flows through us as we meditate is experienced as playing its own part in the simply given miracle of the present moment.

What must be dealt with, however, are those thoughts that are experienced as carrying us away from the concrete immediacy of our body-grounded awareness in the present moment. These are thoughts that we more appropriately categorize as distractions. To meditate even for a few minutes is to experience the phenomena of distracting thoughts. We are sitting still and straight, intending to be present, open, and awake to all that arises in the present moment, when, before we know it, a thought carries us away from our awareness of the present moment. Lost in the thought that has claimed our attention, we are gone!

Actually, it is not that a certain kind of thought, with certain inherent kidnapping qualities, carries us away. Rather, it is truer to say that as a thought comes unexpectedly down the path we, in our attachment to its contents, jump out of the bushes and mug it! As it passes, it drags us off, by virtue of our clinging to it or fighting with it with all our might. As soon as we become aware that we are drifting off into thinking, we are to let go of identifying with thought by gently returning to a sustained stance of being present, open, and awake, neither clinging to nor rejecting anything.

At first, and for quite some time, we tend to drift off into this or that thought before we are aware we are doing so. It is only after the fact that we realize we have once again so overly identified with conceptual thinking as to lose our body-grounded awareness of the present moment. Each time this occurs we are to simply renew our interior stance of being present, open, and awake, neither clinging to nor rejecting anything. As our practice ripens we become less and less subject to drifting off into this or that thought. We learn to remain more firmly established in a body-grounded wakefulness, observing each thought as it arises, endures, and passes away.

While traveling in Asia I was privileged to have a dialogue with the Venerable Bunchit, a Theravada Buddhist monk in Bangkok, Thailand. We discussed the meditative stance of cultivating a sustained awareness of all that arises, endures, and passes away. As he expressed it, in meditation one simply sits, aware of each thought, emotion, and sensation as it arises, remaining aware of it without judgment until it dissipates. As it dissipates one continues sitting as the next thought, emotion, or sensation arises, remaining aware of it without judgment until it dissipates.

I asked if he would consider sitting in this manner to be a way of experiencing impermanence directly. He said yes. I asked if he would consider experiencing impermanence directly as the beginnings of enlightenment. He said yes. When we sit in meditation present, open, and awake to the flux and flow of our own mind, we enter into a direct experience of the impermanent nature of the self, one with the impermanent nature of the ceaselessly flowing present moment. To sit in this flow, surrendering to it utterly, dying to all possessive illusions of an autonomous, permanent self apart from this flow, is to open ourselves to a direct experience of the infinite presence we call God manifested in this very flow of this very moment in which we sit.

And so, as we meditate, we are to do our best to remain quietly steadfast in the awareness of each thought arising, enduring and passing away, without drifting away from the immediacy of present moment before thinking begins. This directive is to be maintained regardless of the content of the thought that arises. The thought that seemingly carries us off into thinking may be something quite mundane. We are sitting there being as present as we can be in the present moment when suddenly, before we know it, we are in the oatmeal we had earlier this morning—how good it was, how next time we will try to remember to put raisins in it. Without rejecting the idea of oatmeal, without rejecting ourselves for having drifted off into thoughts about oatmeal, we, in fidelity to the present moment attentiveness of our practice, are to simply let go of the thought about oatmeal by renewing our stance of remaining present, open, and awake in the immediacy of the present moment.

The thought that seemingly carries us away may be of something quite unpleasant—a sudden flash of some particularly painful memory or some disturbing event that must be faced in the future. Or the thought that seemingly carries us off may be of some pleasurable or fulfilling aspect of some past or future event. Whether the thoughts be pleasant or unpleasant, the single-minded consistency of the meditation practice remains the same. As soon as we become aware that we have once again become so lost in thought as to have lost awareness of the concrete immediacy of the present moment, we are to simply reinstate a stance of being present, open, and awake in the immediacy of the present moment. We are to be simply aware that we have once again become unaware. We are to be simply aware of all that arises, endures, and passes away as being the all encompassing mystery we seek manifesting itself in and as the simply given miracle of all that arises, endures, and passes away.

The fundamental rule of meditation practice regarding thoughts applies as well to all thoughts about God. While sitting in meditation we may have the most profound thought about God that we have ever had in our life up to that moment. In fidelity to the childlike purity of our practice we are not to reject the idea of God, nor are we to cling to it. But rather, simply be aware of it, allowing it dissipate of its own accord, as we continue leaning into the depths of childlike attentiveness beyond thought. For no idea of God is God. Every idea of God is infinitely less than God. Even a true, revealed idea of God is infinitely less than God.

Ultimately, we are not created by God to think about God, but rather are created by God for God beyond all ideas of God. Therefore, no matter how profound, lofty, and moving a thought about God arising in meditation might be, we are to neither cling to nor reject it, but rather simply be aware of it, allowing it to arise, endure, and pass away. When we meditate we are not trying to have thoughts about God. Rather, we are seeking to realize our eternal oneness with the unthinkable immensity of God, manifested in and as the immediacy of who we simply are, one with all the present moment simply is.

The following story might help to clarify the limitations of conceptual knowledge, particularly when allowed to stand in the way of more intimate, interior modes of knowing, germane to contemplative experience. Imagine a woman who marries a psychologist. On their twenty-fifth wedding anniversary he gives her a present. It is a book entitled *You*, which he explains, he has been secretly writing about her during their twenty-five years of marriage. As she lifts the heavy volume from the box, he points out to her, with a sense of satisfaction in his voice, that when she turns to the back of the book she will find that she is completely indexed. Anything she wants to know about herself, she can just look up! In seeing the book and in hearing how unaware he is of what intimacy is about, she cannot hide her feelings of disappointment and hurt. Seeing her negative reaction, he becomes dismayed and crestfallen, for he has already secretly begun work on their golden anniversary present, a three volume work about their relationship entitled *Us*, completely cross-referenced with the *You* volume!

What the man in this story was doing with his wife is what we, in our ignorance, tend to do with our life. In our tendency to obsess over what we think is the meaning of it all, we forget that no idea of us is us. No idea of the beloved is the beloved. No idea of God is God. No idea of the earth is the earth. No idea of the all encompassing totality of reality in which we and God and others and the earth are one is that totality. No index of theological, philosophical, psychological, or any other category of ideas about reality is the unthinkable mystery of reality prior to and beyond all that thought attains. Realizing this is so, we sit in meditation, not rejecting the thoughts that arise, but rather courageously passing beyond our customary reliance on thought.

What has been said concerning the thoughts that arise in meditation can be said as well of the emotions that are experienced during meditation. As we sit in meditation we experience the entire spectrum of emotions. Sitting still and straight, feeling each emotion as it arises, endures, and passes away, we are awakened to the Godly nature of our life manifested in and as the visceral mystery of sadness, happiness, and all the emotions that rise up within us.

What must be dealt with in meditation, however, is our tendency to cling to or reject the emotions we experience, such that present moment attentiveness is compromised or lost altogether. As soon as we become aware that this is happening, we are to renew our intention of being present, open, and awake, neither clinging to nor rejecting the emotion that we are experiencing. In this open, non-reactive stance, the flow of our fluctuating feelings can continue on, unimpeded by our reactivity. If, for example, a feelings of sadness arises, we are not to reject or become lost in the feeling. Rather we are to simply feel the sadness, being fully present to it as it arises, endures, and passes away, giving rise to the next emotion, which, in turn arises, endures, and passes away.

This undifferentiated openness to and detachment from all emotions pertains as well to all the spiritual consolations and experiences of God's presence that may occur as we meditate. For just as no thought about God is God so, too, no feeling of God is God. Every feeling of God's presence, every spiritual consolation and gift, is infinitely less than the infinite Presence that each thought and emotion manifests.

Sitting in meditation embodies the contemplative wisdom of realizing that if we cling to any experience of God, our possessive attitude leaves us with but a feeling, infinitely less than God. On the other hand, if we sit present, open, and awake to all the experiences of God that may grace our meditation practice, we come to realize these experiences to be God manifested in and as the sheer immediacy of all that we experience.

Just as we are not to cling to consolations, spiritual gifts, and all forms of experiencing God's presence, so, too, we are not to become disheartened by our experiences of spiritual aridity. We are not to reject those times when meditation seems arduous and void of any spiritual value or meaning. Rather, we are to be present, open, and awake to spiritual aridity, allowing it to arise, endure, and pass away, as it plays out its own part in the flux and flow of the divinity of what just is. At the level of ego we, of course, understandably prefer consolation over aridity. As our practice matures, however, we begin to appreciate times of God's apparent absence as times of growing stronger in the awareness that God's apparent absence is itself a modality of God's presence. In a stance of accepting our times of spiritual aridity, we learn what only poverty and helplessness can teach concerning the always surprising and mysterious ways of our ongoing, contemplative self-transformation into God.

How strange it might seem at first to give ourselves over to this simple practice of "tilling the empty fields"[14] of unthinking wakefulness! But from the vantage point of contemplative awareness, what seems strange is that the unthinkable immediacy of the present moment has become the land we know not. Strange and scary, too, that we could go through our whole life and not know something as foundational as the Godly nature of who we really are, one with all the present moment really is. So much of the contemplative path has about it this strange mixture of perplexity and self-evident clarity. Even as we sit in meditation, perplexed and bewildered, deeper down we know and trust that we are finding our way home to an intimate awakening to the divinity of what just is.

Repetition of a Word or Phrase

We have already noted how sitting still, sitting straight, and all aspects of meditation are modalities of the self-transforming directive of being present, open, and awake, neither clinging to nor rejecting anything. We will now explore yet another modality of mindfulness; namely, the repetition of a word or phrase.

The word or phrase you decide to use may be taken from scripture or a favorite hymn or perhaps may be one that comes to you as intuitively resonating with your own childlike attentiveness to the depths. A method of combining the use of a word or phrase with the breath that I personally find helpful is to silently say, "I love you" with each exhalation, as an expression of your whole being as act of love to God. Then, with each inhalation, listen to God saying, "I love you." Each time you drift off into thinking or daydreaming, simply return to this interior, "I love you. . . . I love you," attentiveness to the divinity of the present moment.

In similar fashion the Jesus prayer as taught in the Hesychastic tradition of Orthodox Church[15] combines the breath with the words of the prayer, "Lord Jesus Christ, Son of God, have mercy on me a sinner." With each inhalation one silently says, "Lord Jesus Christ, Son of God," expressive of one's intention of breathing in the presence of the risen Jesus. With each exhalation one silently says, "have mercy on me a sinner," as embodying an interior stance of breathing out all that separates one from Christ. As the practice deepens, the words of the prayer naturally tend to shorten to, "Lord Jesus Christ, have mercy on me," then to, "Lord Jesus Christ," and finally in deep practice, to a barely whispered, "Jesus." In time and with God's grace, the words the prayer descend from the head to the heart, where they awaken an habitual contemplative awareness of God's presence in the midst of one's daily living.

In some traditions the word or phrase is used as a mantra that is repeated with each breath, without stopping. Submitting to the power of the word, as used in this way, embodies the death to egocentric consciousness in which one enters into graced awareness transcending thought. In other traditions, the word or phrase is not said repeatedly without stopping but rather is said only as needed each time one realizes one is drifting or has already drifted away from present moment attentiveness.

Instead of simply describing various ways in which a word or phrase might be used in meditation, we can attempt to move in closer to give a more intimate sense of how a word or phrase might possibly be experienced as a medium of contemplative self-transformation. To this end I will first quote from the seventh chapter of

The Cloud of Unknowing and then explore the practical guidance it offers concerning the use of a word in meditation, particularly with respect to the power of a word to break free of the tyranny of thought. The anonymous author of *The Cloud of Unknowing* writes:

> If you want to gather all your desire into one simple word that the mind can easily retain, choose a short word rather than a long one. A one syllable word such as "God" or "love" is best. But choose one that is meaningful to you. Then fix it in your mind so that it will remain there come what may. . . . Should some thought go on annoying you, demanding to know what you are doing, answer with this one word alone. If your mind begins to intellectualize over the meaning and connotations of this little word, remind yourself that its value lies in its simplicity. Do this and I assure you these thoughts will vanish. Why? Because you have refused to develop them with arguing.[16]

Imagine that you are sitting in meditation and that the simple word you have chosen to sustain present moment attentiveness is the word "God." As you sit in meditation, a discouraging thought arises. You sit watching it arise, endure, and pass away in the flow of a deepening awareness of the divinity of all that arises endures and passes away. But then the discouraging thought begins to engage you in such a way that present moment attentiveness begins to dissipate and become lost all together. The discouraging thought that tries to engage you may be something like, "I do not think you are going to get very far." The wise counsel of *The Cloud of Unknowing* advises not to get into a discussion with discouraging thoughts. If you do you will become discouraged. This is who discouraged people are—people who listen to discouraging thoughts, giving them the imaginary power to name who they are and what their life is about.

Instead, turn to this discouraging thought and say, with silent unwavering resolve, "God!" Answer with this one word alone as often as the discouraging thought distracts you from your sustained stance of contemplative awareness of each thought arising, enduring, and passing away. Answer with this one word alone until the self that has and is discouraging thoughts dies in the emptiness in which you wait in a naked intent for God as he is in himself.

What is true of discouraging thoughts is true of all thoughts, regardless of their content. As they arise, endure, and pass away, we are simply to be aware of their arising, enduring, and passing away in the flow of a deepening awareness of the divinity of all that arises, endures, and passes away. But as soon as any thought begins to engage us in thinking, such that present moment attentiveness begins to dissipate, we can use our word as our singular way of reinstating ourselves in childlike, contemplative wakefulness of the unthinkable divinity of the present moment.

Sitting in this way, a discouraging thought might be followed by a confusing thought, such as "shouldn't you be out helping people or doing something practical? Just what are you trying to achieve by this, really?" The author of *The Cloud* advises not to get in a discussion with confusing thoughts. To do so is to become confused. This is who confused people are—people who listen to confusing thoughts, giving them the imaginary power to name who they are and what their life is about. Instead, look this confusing thought right in the eye and say with singular resolve, "God." Answer with this one word alone as often as the confusing thought arises, until the self that has and is confusing thoughts dies in the emptiness in which you wait for God.

You sit a little longer and a biblical thought comes into the room, engaging you in ways that dissipate present moment attentiveness. The distracting biblical thought might come as a biblical passage, perhaps John 1:1 or Romans 8:3. Do not get into a discussion with a biblical thought or you will become biblical! Being biblical in this pejorative sense means to seize hold of scripture as a conceptual ideology capable of adequately defining or describing God and the way to reach him. This is who people top heavy with biblical thoughts are—people who have listened to and seized hold of biblical thoughts in this reductionistic and possessive manner. As a remedy for this brand of ignorance, sit in the silent attentiveness of meditation and as each biblical thought arises, look the biblical thought right in the eye and say, "God." Answer with this one word alone as often as the biblical thought arises, until the self that has and is biblical thoughts dies in the emptiness in which you wait for God.

You sit a little longer and a Christian, Jewish, or Buddhist thought comes into the room and starts to pull you away from present moment attentiveness by engaging you in thoughts germane to whatever your particular religious tradition might be. Do not get into a discussion with a religious thought or you will become religious, which in this present context means falling under the spell of an ideological answer system, hermetically sealed off from the unthinkable divinity of the present moment. This is who people top heavy with the thoughts of their own religious tradition are—people who listen to religious thoughts, giving them an imaginary power to definitively name who God is and what all life is about. Instead, look the religious thought right in the eye and say, "God." Answer with this one word alone as often as the religious thoughts arise, and the self that has and is religious thoughts dies in the emptiness in which you wait for God.

You sit a little longer and a mystical thought comes into the room and starts pulling you away from present moment attentiveness with some thought about no thought, or some other mystical sounding thought beyond the power of thought to grasp. Do not get into a discussion with mystical thoughts, for if you do you will become mystical. In this context, becoming mystical means taking on a mystical identity as one who goes about thinking mystical things capable of defining or describing the ultimately undefinable, indescribable nature of the divinity of what just is. This is who people top heavy with mystical thoughts are, people who listen to mystical thoughts, giving them an imaginary power to name who they are and what all life is about. Instead look the mystical thought right in the eye and say, "God." As often as mystical thoughts arise answer with this one word alone, and the self that has and is mystical thoughts dies in the emptiness in which you wait for God.

You sit a little longer and a publishable thought comes into the room, and starts pulling you away from present moment attentiveness by saying something publishable about present moment attentiveness. Do not get into a discussion with publishable thoughts or you will become publishable. To be publishable in this pejorative sense means to be someone who walks about with thoughts imagined to be so profound and insightful as to adequately define or describe the ineffable nature of reality. This is who people buzzing with publishable thoughts are, people who listen to publishable thoughts, giving them an imaginary power to name who they are and what all life is about. Instead, look the publishable thought right in the eye and say, "God." As often as publishable thoughts arise, answer with this one word alone, and the self that has and is publishable thoughts dies in the emptiness in which you wait for God. Whatever you do, do not interrupt your meditation session by getting out of your chair to walk across the room or roll off your prayer cushion to crawl on your hands and knees to the nearest writing pad to write down the publishable thought so you do not forget it. For if you do God will strike you on your tush with lightning!

Now, in reality, thank God, nothing happens to any of these things. In fidelity to the transforming effects of our meditation practice we remain at times confused and discouraged. We remain religious and mystical and all else that makes being human so delightfully and painfully human. But the point is that all these things lose their imagined power to name who we are. In this cessation of the self-imposed tyranny of each passing thought and emotional state, contemplative experience awakens, disclosing the all encompassing mystery of God manifested in and as each passing thought and emotion, manifesting who we simply are, one with all the present moment simply is.

Compassion

The theme of compassionate love as a dimension of our contemplative self-transformation has been and will be referred to frequently in these reflections. With respect to meditation practice specifically, we have seen how sitting still with all our heart exposes our limitations in stillness. Compassionately embracing and accepting these limitations awakens us to the eternal stillness of God, one with us in our powerlessness. Sitting straight, deeply relaxed yet wide awake, occasions a descent down through all the layers of our remembered past. When compassionately embraced and accepted, these memories reveal our whole life up till now as permeated through and through with the compassionate love of God.

Sitting in childlike mindfulness of each inhalation giving way to each exhalation giving way to each inhalation awakens us to the enigmatic equality of all forms of birth and death. Surrendering ourselves over to this enigmatic equality, we experience the oceanic compassion in which we, in the midst of our being born and dying, dying and being born, rest invincibly secure. Sitting, gazing with eyes of compassion into our mercurial heart, our gaze embodies the divine gaze of love in which our lives subsist. Sitting, given over to the simple intention of being present, open, and awake, neither clinging to nor rejecting anything, we discover ourselves clinging to and rejecting everything. By freely choosing to be compassionate toward ourselves in our ineptness in present moment attentiveness, our awareness toward ourselves is intimately realized to embody God's compassionate stance toward us as invincibly precious and whole in the midst of our powerlessness.

Up to a point, compassionate love is and must be a conscious choice. Sitting still and straight in meditation, experiencing directly our ineptness in present moment attentiveness, we must freely choose to renew again and again a compassionate stance toward ourselves as precious in our ineptness in present moment attentiveness. This perpetually renewed willingness to be compassionately present to ourselves enlarges our heart and breathes a more expansive lightness into the dark density of our egocentricity. Of course, as actually experienced in meditation and in daily life, this process of establishing ourselves in an habitual stance of compassionate love takes place in the context of countless failures to be compassionate. But this proves to be no hindrance as long as we commit ourselves to being compassionate toward ourselves in our failings to be compassionate. Approached in this way, even our failures to be compassionate prove to be but new opportunities to be compassionate. This process of yielding to compassionate love unfolds and deepens over a lifetime of learning that when all is said and done, love is the playing field where we most truly meet ourselves and others as we really are, precious in our collective frailty.

As we continue to sit in meditation, repeatedly renewing a compassionate stance toward ourselves as precious and one with God in the midst of our frailty, we come to realize that compassion is not simply nor primarily an attitude of our own making. That is to say, compassion does not originate with our free decision to be compassionate. Rather, our free decision to be compassionate is our free decision to yield to compassion flowing through us. In the moment of yielding to compassion flowing through us, we intimately taste something of our essential nature, one with the compassionate nature of the all encompassing mystery of God.

This self-transcending realization of ourselves being invincibly one with the compassionate nature of the mystery we seek is achieved in meditation, occasioning a wondrous passage through a seemingly impassable barrier. The barrier is our ignorance, consisting of all that hinders our awareness of our invincible oneness with the mystery we seek, wholly poured out and identified with us as precious in our ignorance. Meditation brings us into direct contact with the barrier of ignorance. Meditation makes us struggle with it until we exhaust completely any means we can devise to overcome it. Then, just as all seems lost, the passage through the seemingly impassable barrier occurs as an intimate realization that our powerlessness is powerlessness to diminish in any way our oneness with the mystery "beating in our very blood whether we want it to or not."

The more deeply we experience our invincible oneness with the compassionate nature of the mystery we seek, the more impelled we are to be compassionate toward ourselves, others and all living beings. In obeying this impulse to be compassionate, we obey our true nature, one with the compassionate nature of God. We awaken to the secret of all the saints, the secret everybody deep down already knows: that when all is said and done, only love and all that is given in love is real.

Each form of meditation, sincerely and whole-heartedly practiced, gravitates toward the event of passing through the seemingly impassable barrier in which we taste directly our essential oneness with the compassionate nature of the mystery we seek. For each method of meditation, sincerely and wholeheartedly practiced, proves to be our teacher, informing us as gently and lovingly as possible that we are beyond human help. Which is to say, each form of meditation sincerely and wholeheartedly practiced has the potential of teaching us that we cannot by means of our own ego deliver ourselves from our egocentricity. Thus, the paradoxical effectiveness of all methods of meditation is that none of them are effective in the ways we, in our egocentricity, tend at first to imagine. In the beginning we are inclined to sit with an enthusiastic commitment to mastering a chosen method of meditation. But if the commitment is as deep and long as life itself, our initial assumptions give way to the sobering realization that we are powerless to will ourselves into authentic union with the divine mystery beyond the power of the will to achieve. Our initial assumptions about one day finally grasping the prize of divine union give way to the sobering realization that we are powerless to grasp the all encompassing totality that is already perfectly present in and as all that we can and cannot grasp.

If we just keep sitting, day by day, like an unlearned child, yielding to a seemingly endless falling away of every possible foundation on which to establish anything whatsoever, the oceanic compassion that was always there comes flooding into our awareness. We are amazed and filled with joy to discover that the more solidly our meditation practice is established in love, the more surely we advance in the midst of our powerlessness to advance.

Any method of meditation, sincerely practiced, has the potential of occasioning the wondrous passage through the seemingly impassable barrier of our ignorance. But perhaps singling out and exploring the intimate unfoldings of a single method of meditation will help to clarify just how this is so. The method I will focus on is the Zen meditation practice of counting the breaths up to ten:[17] The practice begins in inhaling slowly and deeply, wholly mindful of inhaling slowly and deeply; then holding your breath for just a moment, wholly mindful of holding your breath for just a moment; then exhaling slowly and completely, wholly mindful of exhaling slowly and completely; silently saying as you do so, "one," wholly mindful of silently saying one. The practice continues as, in one unbroken thread of sustained awareness, you continue investing yourself in a childlike, wholehearted absorption of each breath on up to ten. When you drift off into this or that thought, go back to one. When you drift off into sleepiness or daydreaming, go back to one. If you lose count, go back to one. If you notice that the inner utterance of a number is not wholehearted, clear and precise, but vague and half-aware, go back to one. If you get to ten, go back to one.

Just sit, given over to the simple intention of sustained absorption in the immediacy of the present moment, concretized in being wholly absorbed in each breath, each number. Just sit like this in a perpetual willingness to go back to one. Just sit like this letting each instance of returning to one be a renewed stance of compassion for yourself as precious in your ineptness at present moment attentiveness. Just sit this way, with all your heart, knowing and trusting that by way of this compassionate presence the great way is being perfectly manifested.

Do not run away, but instead continue sitting, allowing yourself to be humbled in the crumbling away of any hope of attainment founded upon your own powers. Just keep sitting in the growing awareness of your powerlessness, until your powerlessness unexpectedly opens out onto a starkly beautiful wilderness that is not even on the map the ego-self has been using in its seemingly hopeless expedition into the ineffable. This wilderness is God's secret place hidden from all eternity right before your eyes. It is here you come to discover that the true purpose of meditation is not to get to ten, to nine, or for that matter even to two, for to strive to get to two as some kind of attainment is to fall prey to the illusion of attainment. It is to fall prey to our ignorance, in which we imagine there is anything to attain that is not already perfectly given in and as the concrete immediacy of who we simply are, one with all the present moment simply is.

It is in the stark wilderness of a perpetual willingness to go back to one that you come to realize that all things are possible for the one who learns how to go back to the vast, virginal, inexhaustible nature of one—the numerical cipher of our humility. It is in the stark wilderness of a perpetual willingness to go back to one that you come to realize that God has her way with the one who has learned to go back to one. One is just a hair's breadth from zero—the numerical cipher of the abyss-like no-thing-ness of God, wholly poured in and as the abyss-like nature of who we simply are, one with all the present moment simply is. Perhaps with a subtle smile, perhaps with a great big laugh, perhaps with tears streaming down your face, perhaps with nothing at all but your childlike willingness to head back one more time to the inexhaustible and fount-like nature of one, you taste directly your oneness with the overflowing generosity of God's compassionate presence.

Here's another way of putting it. Our egocentric self sets out with an egocentric understanding of what it means to be free of the tyranny of egocentricity. This egocentric understanding is that of having to jump over a bar that is set so high that only the most finely tuned spiritual athlete could ever hope to clear it. Our struggles with distractions, sleepiness and indifference brings us to a point of near despair, convincing us that our doubts were true concerning our inability to master such a seemingly unreachable challenge. Then, just as we are spent in the futility of investing ourselves in our own illusions concerning the nature of the fulfillment that alludes us, the saving event happens. Love steps out and places the bar flat on the ground! Approaching the bar, disoriented by the unthinkable simplicity of the task, we trip over it, falling headlong into God, wholly poured out in and as who we simply are—all precious in our fragility, strangely whole and one with God in the midst of our fragmentation.

Walking Meditation

Our reflections on meditation as a path of self-transformation would be incomplete without going on to explore walking meditation. The directives for walking mediation presented and explored in this section are based on what I have learned in my exposure to the walking meditation practices of Buddhism. I was first exposed to Zen meditation by Thomas Merton as a novice at Gethsemani Abbey. But I did not have first hand exposure to the Zen tradition of walking meditation until the mid-nineteen eighties when I was invited to be one of the Christian faculty members at the Buddhist-Christian conference at the Naropa Institute in Boulder, Colorado. The first year I participated in this conference, I attended a session led by the Zen master Eido Roshi. He began the session by briefly presenting the fundamentals of sitting meditation practice. We then sat in silence for about twenty five minutes of sitting meditation. He then introduced the fundamentals of walking meditation, after which we all stood and walked together in a long slow, silent procession around the circumference of the room.

Religious exercises that included walking were, at this point, by no means completely new to me. As a Catholic I had participated many times in liturgical processions and in the devotional practice of making the stations of the cross. In the monastery I would frequently walk alone in the cloister, simply trying to be mindfully present to each step. And I had experienced on many occasions the liberating power of walking in the midst of nature. But it was not until that day at Naropa that I experienced walking so slowly and mindfully in a manner so directly continuous with the silent stillness of sitting meditation.

Walking slowly in silent mindfulness, single file around the room with Buddhists and fellow Christians was a powerful experience for me of the ecumenical potential of contemplative spirituality. While there was an obvious awareness of and respect for the differences between Christianity and Buddhism, there was also a communal awareness of encountering each other at a level that preceded and transcended those differences.

An exposure to the Vipassana[18] Buddhist traditions of walking meditation occurred more recently on a trip with my wife, Maureen, to Bangkok and Sri Lanka, where I had the opportunity to practice walking meditation with Buddhist monks and lay people. In my one-on-one interviews with the monks, I tried as best as I could to comprehend their responses to my questions about meditation practice, enlightenment, and nirvana. But in meditating together there was no need to comprehend anything. We sat and walked together as one in the white light of contemplative awareness of the Mystery prior to the point at which it begins to give itself, whole and complete, in each tradition of the spectrum of contemplative traditions. Even more fundamental than these ecumenical considerations is that at both Naropa and in Asia I experienced in the slow, mindful walking a rudimentary form of contemplation in action. In the walking I discovered a way to allow the deep stillness fostered in sitting meditation to flow out, unbroken and uninterrupted, into bodily movement.

As with the directives given for sitting meditation, the directives for walking meditation are presented here with the assumption that you will be discerning the degree and manner in which they may or may not apply to you. You may want to incorporate some form of walking meditation into your practice of centering prayer or some other Christian contemplative prayer or meditation practice. Or you may want to practice walking meditation as an integral component of learning Zen or Vipassana meditation methods, in which case you will want to seek out an authorized teacher in these traditions. Or you may want simply to allow some of the insights shared here to illumine your present experience of walking outdoors in the midst of nature, awake to and appreciative of the miracle of simply being alive in the world. The point is that I will be sharing with you here some simple directives for walking meditation which will hopefully serve as a starting point from which you can allow your own unique ways of practicing walking meditation to emerge and develop.

I will first present some basic directives for walking meditation. Then I will demonstrate how walking meditation naturally dovetails with both sitting meditation and with learning to habituate a state of contemplative mindfulness of the tasks of daily living. Finally, mention will be made of the self-transforming effects of practicing walking meditation with others.

Most people find walking meditation is best performed barefooted or in their stocking feet. You may, however, prefer to leave your shoes on. Begin by standing straight and still, breathing slowly and naturally, with your eyes lowered toward the ground. Hold your arms and hands in any position that feels natural and comfortable. You might, for example, have your arms extended straight downward at your sides with your hands relaxed, or with your fingers extended and your palms facing forward. It might feel most natural for you to walk with your arms down, and your hands clasped behind your back. Or you might naturally follow the Zen tradition of making a fist with one hand, then folding the other hand over it, and holding both hands in front of you at the level of your stomach. Or you may find it most natural to join your palms in front of you, fingers extended in a position of prayer.

Stand still and straight, eyes lowered toward the ground, breathing slowly and naturally, absorbed in the whole hearted awareness of simply standing. Standing in this way with deep devotion is itself a deep practice, one empowered to awaken an intimate realization of the divinity of standing.

When it feels interiorly right to begin your first step, shift your weight to your right leg. Lift your left foot slowly and mindfully off the ground and slowly move it forward, lowering it to the ground about half a foot length ahead of your right foot. Then, in one continuous, slow movement, shift your weight to your left leg. Neither pausing nor rushing, slowly begin lifting your right foot off the ground. Move it slowly forward and lower it about half a foot length ahead of your left foot. Walk on like this, in one slow, continuous movement.

The essence of the practice is childlike mindfulness of each step. As you lift your foot be wholeheartedly absorbed in lifting your foot. As you slowly swing your foot forward, be wholeheartedly absorbed in swinging your foot forward. As you lower your foot to the ground, be wholeheartedly absorbed in lowering your foot to the ground. As your foot makes contact with the ground, be quietly absorbed in your foot touching the ground.

If you find it helpful, you can use a word or phrase with each step. Each time your foot touches the ground, you might silently say, "Jesus," "God," "life," or "love." Or you can say a phrase with each step. In the Christian Zen retreat I attended led by the Jesuit priest Hans

Koenen, he suggested using the phrase from scripture, "make straight the way of the Lord." You could silently say, "I love you" as you lift your foot and begin swinging it forward, and then listen to God saying, "I love you," as you continue swinging your foot forward and touching it to the earth. If you are accustomed to using a word or phrase in your sitting meditation, you are likely to find that word or phrase to be the most natural word to continue using in the walking meditation as well. ·

The word or phrase that feels most natural to you might be expressed as a question. For example, each time your foot touches the ground, you might silently ask, "What is this?" Or as you lift your foot up off the ground and begin moving it forward, your question might be, "What is this leaving behind?" As you move your foot forward and begin touching it to the ground your question might be, "What is this moving on?" The conceptual mind is, of course, ready to jump in, suggesting the answer to such questions might be "God," or "the mystery I seek," or "the all encompassing totality of reality," or "the direct expression of the perpetual flux and movement of the cosmic dance." But as we walk, the questions neither arise from nor are directed to our conceptual mind. Rather, the questions serve to awaken us to the concrete immediacy of our whole-hearted absorption in each step as being nothing less or other than the all encompassing mystery we seek manifested in and as this step . . . this step . . . this step.

If you find it helpful to do so, you can consciously incorporate your breathing into your walking by inhaling deeply and slowly as you lift your foot and begin moving it forward, then exhaling as you continue to move it forward and lower it to the ground. If you are saying a word or phrase as part of your practice, you may find that it tends to blend naturally with the breath. Do not try and juggle all these various possibilities at once, but simply begin walking with childlike mindfulness of each step, gently exploring over time the ways in which breath awareness and the repetition of a word or phrase might possibly enhance your walking meditation practice.

The walking should have a natural, flowing quality. Do not stop between each step. Do not lift your foot in an exaggerated movements, as if yanking your foot out of a mud hole. Do not lift each leg high into the air in exaggerated movements, as if you were wearing snow shoes. Do not walk with an aura of impatience. But rather, walk slowly and naturally in an even, flowing movement that embodies your childlike mindfulness of each step. Move as a huge old fish slowly moves through primordial waters. Move as a glacier moves across the land. Move as one who is awakening to the eternal stillness flowing out, unbroken and uninterrupted in and as one's foot lifting up, swinging forward, and touching the earth.

If you are practicing walking meditation alone at home, you might decide to walk slowly around the room. Walking in a circle embodies the circularity of life's journey, in which we move out from God and, without ever leaving God, follow the long slow curve of our life that leads us through death back to God. The configuration of the room or your personal inclination may prompt you to walk back and forth in straight line. If this proves to be the case, walk in a straight line until you come to the wall. When you get to the wall, stop, mindful and attentive to the divinity manifested every time we come up to point beyond which we cannot pass. Stand still with all your heart, allowing your standing to incarnate your faith in the divinity of standing. When it intuitively feels right, begin lifting your foot, turning it slowly about a quarter turn, and lowering it to the ground. Continue lifting and lowering each foot in the contemplative practice of turning about, mindful of this turning as embodying the divinity of all the times we turn about. When the turn is completed and you are facing back the way you came, stand motionless in mindful attentiveness of the divinity manifested in all the times we find ourselves heading back the way we came. When it intuitively feels right to do so, slowly lift your left foot, beginning your walk back across the space you came. In other words, when walking back and forth, do not let times of stopping and turning about be interruptions in your walking but rather integral aspects of an unbroken and flowing process.

When walking very slowly in the manner described above, we are repeatedly balancing ourselves on one leg as we move the other leg forward. In doing so we sometimes wobble a little as we lose our balance. This occasional wobbling plays its own part in walking meditation. As our sincere mindfulness of each step ripens, we will glimpse in each faltering step, the art form of contemplative living as a process of learning to wobble well. By this is meant, learning to waver with compassionate awareness of ourselves and of all people as ineffably elegant and precious in all our wavering ways.

Walking meditation naturally dovetails with sitting meditation. For most of us, most of the time sitting in meditation for twenty to twenty-five minutes is long enough to settle into the meditative state while at the same time being short enough to honor the arduous aspects of sitting motionless for long periods. Sometimes, however, it is just as a twenty to twenty-five minute session of sitting meditation is coming to an end that we begin to feel ourselves going deeper into a sustained state of body-grounded mindfulness of the divinity of the present moment. At such times, to stop meditating feels a bit like walking out of a play in the middle of the second act. It hardly seems right, and yet to go on much longer might not seem quite right either with respect to the importance of not pushing beyond our limits relative to the arduous aspects of sitting motionless for extended periods of time. Walking meditation provides a way of compassionately integrating the arduous aspects of sitting meditation with the felt need to give ourselves more time in which to allow the meditative state to deepen and expand. Sitting motionless for a full hour may be a bit too much for most of us. But sitting for twenty-five minutes, practicing walking meditation for ten minutes and sitting in meditation for another twenty-five minutes provides a balanced and compassionate way of practicing meditation for a full hour.

As each session of sitting meditation comes to an end, questions of contemplative living arise: As I learn to awaken to the divinity of sitting, can I, at the end of this session of meditation learn to stand, awake to the divinity of standing? Can I learn to walk across the room, awake to the divinity of walking across a room? Can I open the door, awake to the divinity manifested every time I open a door? Can I pass someone in the hallway or out on the street awake to the divinity manifested in our every encounter with one another? Walking meditation is a living yes to these questions of contemplative living.

In practicing walking meditation we learn to navigate the transition from stillness to movement without breaking the thread of present moment attentiveness. As we enter into the flowing movement of walking meditation, the unbroken thread of sustained contemplative wakefulness occasions an intimate realization of God, wholly poured out and given over to our foot lifting up, swinging forward, lowering and touching the simply given mystery of the earth.

A clarifying note that can be added at this point is that practicing walking meditation between two periods of sitting meditation can be done briskly in a manner that has very much the same effect as splashing cold water on your face to renew and invigorate your awareness. Brisk walking can be done outdoors around the yard or garden, or indoors around the room or through areas of the house. Walking briskly tends to be shorter than ten minutes in that most people find that just one or two minutes of brisk walking is enough to renew and revitalize their awareness. What matters is that the brisk walking not dissipate but sustain in bodily movement the intimate wakefulness fostered in sitting still.

As we learn to move back and forth between sitting and walking meditation without breaking the thread of present moment attentiveness, we begin to sense the possibility of sustaining contemplative awareness of the present moment in the midst of our daily activities. Monastic life is a contemplative culture that invites a gradual metamorphosis of one's consciousness, such that the daily round of prayer and work are experienced as a single unitive movement of contemplative living. The dictum of Benedictine monasticism *ora et labora*, prayer and work, calls upon the monk or nun to experience prayer and work not as two different activities, one opposed to the other, but as two modes of a single unitive experience of the inherent holiness of daily living. We who are seeking to live a more contemplative way of life in the midst of today's world must cultivate a contemplative culture in our homes and places of employment by creatively finding ways to habituate a contemplative awareness of the inherent holiness of the life we are living.

The following exercise is intended to demonstrate how sitting meditation, walking meditation and the performance of daily tasks might gradually flow together in a habitual state of present moment attentiveness. The exercise consists of first choosing some household chore that needs to be done. I will use, as an example, washing a sink full of dirty dishes. Begin the exercise by first sitting in meditation for about twenty to thirty minutes. Then slowly stand, and walk in a slow mindful manner to the kitchen sink full of dirty dishes. Stand at the sink, mindfully gazing for a moment at the dishes. Slowly and mindfully put soap in the sink. Fill the sink with hot water, attentive to the simple given-ness of the sound of running water. Wash, rinse, and place each item in the drainer with mindfulness. When the dishes are finished, pull the plug, listen to and watch the water going down the drain. Rinse out the sink with mindfulness. Dry each item and put it in its proper place with natural and deliberate mindfulness. Wipe off the counter tops with mindfulness. Then slowly walk back to your place of sitting meditation and sit for another twenty to twenty-five minutes. Then open a journal and begin writing spontaneously and sincerely about what it would be like to live in this way. That is, what would it be like to open and close doors, take some boxes out of the garage, file papers, answer the phone, not as rude interruptions into a carefully sequestered off contemplative life, but, to the contrary, as living embodiments of the hands-on divinity of daily living.

The self-transforming potential of exercises such as the one suggested above can be heightened still further by setting aside retreat days, devoted to the deepening of an habitual state of contemplative awareness of the present moment. Follow the promptings of your heart in what seems most natural and helpful relative to the pacing and number of hours to be spent in sitting and walking meditation. Prepare and eat simple meals with mindfulness. Keep all conversations with others to a minimum. If you journal or read anything at all, read and write in a mindful manner only that which awakens and deepens a sustained state of mindfulness of the divinity of the present moment. Let your prayers be sincere and childlike, with an emphasis on opening yourself to the intimate realization of God manifested in and as the concrete immediacy of each passing moment. As you end your retreat day, ask for the grace of entering back into your daily routines more contemplatively awake and appreciative of the inherent holiness of your daily routines.

At first, and for quite some time, our efforts in being more contemplatively awake to the divinity of each passing moment requires a continually renewed effort. Catching ourselves in the act of rushing we must consciously choose to slow down. Catching ourselves becoming overly reactive to stressful situations, we must choose to breathe into the situation a more genuinely present and compassionate way of engaging in the flow of what is happening. With time, however, this conscious effort transforms the intimate texture of our daily awareness. With time we become ever more habitually awake to the inherent holiness of the one unending moment in which our lives unfold.

Participating in meditation retreats and attending regular sessions of a local meditation group provide the opportunity to practice walking meditation with others. In the meditation intensive retreats that I lead, the participants take part in hour long meditation sessions seated in chairs or on prayer cushions or benches arranged facing inward around the four walls of the room. When the first twenty-five minutes of sitting meditation ends, all stand in silence and walk slowly around the circumference of the room for ten minutes or for one rotation of the room, which ever comes first. Then all sit to complete the hour meditation with another twenty-five minutes of sitting meditation.

Walking together in this way embodies fundamental lessons regarding the communal nature of life's journey. Walking slowly, single-file around the room, you are made aware that you cannot walk faster than the person in front of you. Likewise, walking slowly, single file around the room, you are made aware that all the people behind you cannot walk faster than you. If you start walking slower and slower in becoming so absorbed in your private world of walking that you forget everyone walking with you, a problem begins to develop. Namely, all who are walking with you will begin to pile up behind you. By taking responsibility not to allow the distance between you and the person in front of you to increase, your absorption in each step extends out to embrace a sensitivity to the communal nature of your walking. And walking in a sustained state of awareness of the communal nature of each step in turn evolves into an intimate awareness of the essentially communal nature of the life you are living. Walking together embodies the realization that you cannot authentically live absorbed in your private inner world. The way you walk your daily walk impacts, for better or for worse, those whose lives are inexorably bound up with your own.

When the group's collective practice is deep and strong, walking together in silence can occasion profound realization that the unforeseeable fulfillment we are moving into is always manifesting itself perfectly in and as the journey itself. I was once conducting a meditation retreat in which the participants were practicing sitting and walking meditation in the manner described above. That is, the chairs were arranged facing inward around the four sides of the room. Each hour of meditation consisted of twenty-five minutes of sitting meditation, ten minutes of walking meditation and twenty-five minutes of sitting meditation.

Sitting next me and walking directly behind me was Sister Julian, who had taught my mother in high school. Sister Julian, who was in her eighties at the time, had to use a walker. During the ten minute periods of slowly walking together around the room, the communal silence of the walking was rhythmically woven with her walker, squeaking loudly each time she would move it forward and lean her weight on it to take her next step. I became aware of the sound of her squeaking walker. Then I became aware of my irritation. Then I became aware of being irritated with myself for being irritated. Then I became aware of being irritated with myself that I was still subject to getting irritated at myself for getting irritated. As I entered into the concrete immediacy of simply walking, this egocentric noise slowly fell away and I was left with a deepening, childlike awareness of belonging to a community moving together as one in a silence woven with the squeak, squeak, squeak of Sister Julian's walker.

Childlike fidelity unto death sounds just like this—squeak, squeak, squeak! The long walk into feeble limitations and beyond sounds just like this—squeak, squeak, squeak! The unbearable beauty of a person's unself-aware engagement in the primordial flow of life sounds just like this—squeak, squeak, squeak! The whole journey of life sounds just like this—squeak, squeak, squeak; never, in the end, other than a human being coming to the end, never in the end anything less than the deathless divinity manifested in and as each step we take. This is deep walking. This is God manifested in and as this step . . . this step . . . this step.

Repeated practice of sitting and walking meditation alone, and with others, embodies the interplay of solitude and communion that permeates all of life. It is to this interplay that we will now direct our attention in exploring the directive: Find your contemplative community and enter it.

PART THREE

FIND YOUR CONTEMPLATIVE COMMUNITY
AND ENTER IT

6. Instances of Contemplative Community

Just as finding our contemplative practice and practicing it is vital to contemplative living, so too is finding our contemplative community and entering it. When you first think of contemplative community you are, perhaps, likely to think in terms of finding others who share your desire for a more contemplative way of life. Toward the end of this chapter, and elsewhere in these reflections, we will be touching briefly on this aspect of contemplative community. In this chapter, however, and in the one which follows it, we will be taking a much more fundamental and universal approach to contemplative community. We will be poetically exploring our membership in the unitive mystery of the cosmic dance of God—one with us, one with others, one with the earth that sustains us. Approached at this level, *finding* our contemplative community occurs in each and every granting of contemplative experience in which the all-is-one nature of reality is realized. And *entering* our contemplative community is a life-long process of allowing our contemplative experience of the unitive nature of reality to transform us to the point that we become someone whose life gives witness in the world to the unity of the world which is one with God.

The experience of being a self with boundaries provides a point of view from which we can begin our exploration of our contemplatively realized oneness with the unitive nature of reality. Boundary maintenance is one of the fundamental ways in which we maintain our ongoing sense of security and well being. We have physical, sexual, emotional, intellectual, and spiritual boundaries.[1] If our boundaries in any of these areas are too rigid, we tend to be overly self-protective and isolated. If, on the other hand, our boundaries are too weak in any of these areas, we have difficulties taking care of ourselves in situations that may be harmful, sometimes abusive, or even life-threatening. A healthy sense of one's boundaries is neither too rigid nor too weak, but rather consists of maintaining the balance of allowing into ourselves those influences we rightfully perceive to be self-enhancing as we simultaneously keep out those influences rightfully perceived to be threatening.

The process of boundary maintenance is, in fact, quite complicated as evidenced by how frequently we come to realize that an influence we perceived at the time to be self-enhancing, and so allowed into ourselves, proved, in the light of subsequent experience, to be actually self-destructive. And, inversely, influences perceived at the time to be threatening and kept at bay, proved to be a lost opportunity for self-enhancement. Adding to the complexity is that our ongoing sense of self is also affected by how we maintain our boundaries with respect to all that comes from within—the feeling in the pit of the stomach, the intuitive hunch, the impelling concern that will neither go away nor come into clear view.

To say that boundary maintenance is complex hardly does justice to the personal anguish that can occur in having our boundaries violated by another, by ourselves, by circumstance, or by forces unknown. Likewise, who can calculate the loss incurred in rejecting as harmful someone who simply wanted to love us, or in refusing walk through a door opened by insight or by a dream drawing us in the direction of our deepest longings?

So far we are limiting ourselves primarily to a consideration of maintaining our boundaries with respect to all that has boundaries, that is, with respect to this or that specific person, event, feeling, thought, or set of circumstances as perceived in ego consciousness. Our primary concern in this chapter, however, is that of the self-transforming event of contemplative experience in which we discover ourselves to be subsisting in boundlessness, for boundlessness is that which contemplative experience realizes. We see children playing. The children clearly have boundaries, as do we. And yet in the contemplative glimpsing of the children is the heart's recognition of something about their play, that manifests, unbeknownst to them, the boundless play of the cosmic dance.

The contemplative glimpsing of their play recognizes their play to be boundless in that, in the actual moment in which the contemplative glimpse occurs, we intuitively recognize in their play an overflowing uncircumscribability. There is the intuitive understanding that if we were to draw a circle around the children at play, the mystery their playing manifests would playfully overflow the circumference of the circle. Even if the circle were to be infinite in circumference, its circumference would be playfully and effortlessly breached by their play's boundless nature. Such is the transcendence contemplative experience realizes—a boundlessness that delights in actively overflowing all set boundaries.[2] Like diamonds on sunlit water, like children running down a hill, the uncircumscribable richness of what simply is delights in effortlessly crossing all boundaries with which we might attempt to hem it in.

This boundlessness that playfully overflows all boundaries, overflows into our heart as well in the moment we are contemplatively awakened to it, evoking a litany of questions: If these children are this moment manifesting boundlessness so perfectly, is it possible that all children everywhere in every moment are perfectly manifesting boundlessness? Is it possible that everyone everywhere, everything everywhere is manifesting boundlessness perfectly? Is it possible that I in this moment am manifesting perfectly the boundlessness being manifested to me in these children? Is it possible that I could learn to surrender to this boundlessness and, in surrendering to it, learn to live by this boundlessness, day by day in everything I do and say? And if I make this surrender, what will happen to my customary sense of myself that is perpetuated in my ongoing maintenance of my boundaries? What will become of me if I do not make this surrender, if I do not open myself to the destiny boundlessness beckons me to discover? Do not these very questions, sincerely asked, render me over into boundlessness? Do not these very questions asked out of idle curiosity or the need to be clever constitute a defense against boundlessness as a kind of resistance to its embrace?

The questions flow on and on like a river, like the refrains of a song the rhythms of which are as familiar to us as our own breath. We are on holy ground whenever we give ourselves over to such childlike ponderings born of boundlessness. And it is on this holy ground that I now find myself, that you now find yourself insofar as we have been brought to this present moment of writing and reading these reflections by the incessant lure of the litany of questions boundlessness engenders.

Writing thus, reading thus on this holy ground, let us proceed by way of reflecting on four instances or specific aspects of the contemplative community to which we are awakened in moments of contemplative experience and into which we are called to enter in our ongoing efforts in contemplative living. Reflecting on these four instances will provide an opportunity to summarize and examine in a new light the threefold philosophy of contemplative living with which we began our reflections. It will also, hopefully, help us to become more aware of and responsive to the essentially communal nature of the contemplative path on which we find ourselves.

The first instance is that of the cosmic dance itself that is already perfectly present prior to our being contemplatively awakened to it. Standing full and complete prior to our experience of it, this first instance is a communal mystery that "beats in our very blood whether we want it to or not." It is the mystery "no despair of ours can alter."

It is this first instance that gives our moments of spontaneous contemplative experience the quality akin to that of an explorer, who, after a long and weary trek through a dense forest suddenly comes upon a raging river, the timeless beauty of which enthralls him. The explorer knows the river's raging beauty does not begin with his discovery of it. Rather, his discovery of it is the moment in which he comes upon a timeless beauty already in progress. So too, in our moments of contemplative awakening, we intuitively sense that we have serendipitously stumbled upon an ineffable holiness already in progress. If a philosophy of contemplative living can be said to have a beginning and an end, it is here, where from "before beginningless beginnings, beyond endless ends"[3] the present moment perpetually manifests the unmanifested presence we call God.

In the moment we turn to see a flock of birds descending, is our poor heart—with all its ragged edges, all its boundaries—any less boundless than the birds, which, in their descent, disclose the boundless nature of the cosmic dance? Where do we end and the birds begin? Where do the birds end and we begin? This unity in which, in this moment of contemplative awakening, we realize we and the birds are so forever one, where does it ever begin? Where does it ever end, encircling as it does the timeless, boundless unity of all that is and is not?[4]

The second instance is the lightning crack. It is our being alone on a starlit night, tasting the boundlessness of night. The second instance is our personal experience of the first instance. It is our personal discovery of an already perfectly present mystery. If the first instance refers to the ever-present mystery prior to our experience of it, this second instance refers to our subjective experience of the mystery prior to our responding to it.

We turn to see a flock of birds descending. Before we have a chance to accept or reject it, before we can begin to form our first formulations of what is occurring, we discover a full-blown coup-d'état is already in progress. Boundlessness is already crossing our boundaries. Simplicity itself is already manifesting itself in our simple awareness of what simply is.

It, however, does not quite seem to be the case that in this instantaneous moment of contemplative awakening there is no response whatsoever, for it seems that in this instant of awakening, prior to all conscious willing, there is within us an already-present acceptance of the event of boundlessness crossing our boundaries as that for which we have been waiting all along.

When the eaglet, in the moment of hesitant inevitability, leaps from the nest for the first time into the abyss below, the wind of its free fall meets its outstretched wings with a mighty YES that sends the eagle soaring up into the empty air of its ever present destiny in boundlessness. So, too, with us. In a willing prior to all conscious willing our essential nature meets the contemplative event with a mighty YES that sends us soaring up into the empty air of our ever present destiny in boundlessness.

This yes is not the yes of yes and no. Rather it is the yes of each thing simply being the transparent manifestation of the boundless mystery it manifests. Thus, this yes is the yes of fire rising upwards, the yes of water flowing downward. With the eagle, this yes is that given in its leap into the abyss, in its stretching out its wings so eagle-like above the earth. With us, this yes is given in the ease and naturalness with which we look up to discover the boundlessness of the eagle's soaring crossing our boundaries. And in looking up we discover our own boundless nature to be a beholder of boundlessness, one in whom boundlessness is expressed in and as our boundless experience of it.

What can be said of a willing prior to all conscious willing can be said as well of a knowing prior to all conscious knowing. Even before we have a chance to be bewildered by the incomprehensibility of the contemplative experience of boundlessness crossing our boundaries, we know what is happening. This knowing is not that of forming a conceptual formulation about something. Rather, it is each being knowing how to be the being that it is. It is the primitive knowledge of fire knowing what rising is, of water knowing what flowing is, of an eagle knowing what soaring is. In the instant we look up to discover the boundlessness of the eagle's soaring crossing our boundaries, it is a beholder of boundlessness knowing what the beholding of boundlessness is; and knowing it as a small child, sound asleep, knows without waking up that its father is picking it up and carrying it off to bed.

This second instance of our instantaneous awakening to the boundless nature of the cosmic dance crossing our boundaries does not bring us to anything resembling the annihilation of our boundaries. Rather, it brings us to the transforming realization of the boundless nature of all boundaries, the limitless nature of all limits. To see how this is so, we have but to imagine ourselves in the instantaneous contemplative experience of holding a newborn infant. How limited the infant is! How small! How utterly dependent on us to maintain the boundaries it cannot yet even begin to maintain for itself!

In this moment we intuit the boundless nature of this infant's boundaries, the limitless nature of its limits in intuiting its boundaries and limits to be inherently worthy of a respect, even a reverence that knows no bounds. In its precise littleness, as if meticulously cut out with a razor blade, in its mysterious weight in weighing hardly anything at all, in its imperial strength with which it grasps our extended little finger, it all but carries our heart away. In this moment we know with an invincible certitude that were we to die in the act of trying to save the life of this infant we would die in the truth.

This spontaneous experience of holding a newborn infant helps us to understand an essential dimension of our meditation practice. We sit for hours, weeks, months, years in bare attention of our breath. In the poverty of our practice is granted a contemplative experience of a single breath: How precious life is! How mysteriously it arises breath by breath! Limits? Yes! What is more limited than this breath so small? Hardly anything at all. Yet, how limitless this limit in manifesting so miraculously the sweet marrow of the mystery. Boundaries? Yes! How much clearer could my boundaries be in my being so bound, breath by breath, to this life I am living? Yet, how boundless this boundary in being the way the body embodies the boundless mystery of the cosmic dance. How strangely clear that if I were to die in this moment, this breath would be the point of passing through into the infinity it so ineffably expresses.

To realize the boundless nature of all boundaries, the limitlessness nature of all limits is to realize that the shape and form of everything that is, is the shape and form of the boundless mystery that enraptures us. It is to realize that the fragility of our boundaries is itself the tremulous presence of God, the "dance of the Lord in emptiness" made manifest in and as the fragility of our boundaries.

Here is born the fierce tenderness of the enlightened heart. Tender because a heart so enlightened instinctively avoids all violence toward the precious presence of what simply is. Fierce because a heart so enlightened harbors the mustard seed of divine justice that springs up as the willingness to put one's self on the line whenever or wherever violence is being done to oneself, others, or the earth that sustains us. Here, in short, is born a radical and profound experience of finding one's contemplative community in being contemplatively awakened to one's ineffable communion with the all encompassing totality the present moment manifests.

The third instance consists of the journey of contemplative self-transformation that arises from the depths of divinity to which we are, from time to time, fleetingly awakened. The beginnings of the journey are hidden in our apparent lack of response to our moments of spontaneous contemplative experience. As each moment of contemplative awakening dissipates, we turn and walk away as if no awakening had ever occurred. The gate of heaven opens but we do not enter. The invitation to join in the general dance is received, but is neither recognized nor accepted.

We know what this unenlightened ignorance is like. It is the preoccupation with the dandruff, the hemorrhoids, and the finances; it is being upset that someone forgot to put the lid back on the whatchamacallit, or being upset that someone is upset with you that you, for the one hundredth time, forgot to put the lid back on the whatchamacallit. It is the cold or the heat. It is the rain or the lack of rain. It is the secret worry about the secret problem that shows no signs of going away; the obsessing over what we think is the meaning of it all. It is the living and acting as if our life was made up of nothing but the endless round of all such things. Such is the nature of our unenlightened ignorance, the source of all sorrow, the seedbed of the violence we perpetuate upon ourselves, on others, and on the earth that sustains us.

To recall the story of our own journey up till now is perhaps, to recall how at one time we were buried alive in a pervasive unawareness of the divinity of our daily living. But happily we tell of how we, in our hectic pace, were overtaken by a flock of birds descending into the folly of our ways. We tell the story of how, in having fallen into the abyss of a child's upturned face, we never quite regained our balance in unawareness, as we kept losing our balance, again and again, in other equally commonplace, equally ineffable daily miracles. We tell the story of how these glimpses of the cosmic dance continue to occur, such that we are never able to quite right ourselves in unawareness.

In being perpetually subject to losing our footing again and again in the incomprehensible stature of simple things, we begin to comprehend in some unthinkable way the only way we can proceed. Rather than fight to maintain our balance in ignorance, we must find our balance in the transcendent depths of the concrete immediacy of the present moment. We must yield to the dark ferment of a holy discontent with a life of unenlightened ignorance. We must, in obeying an inner imperative of our awakened heart, become a "pilgrim of the absolute,"[5] one for whom nothing less than the all encompassing totality will do.

The beginnings of the journey of contemplative self-transformation are often marked by a quality of high hopes of immanent success. Committing ourselves to meditation and other contemplative practices, we often begin with a graced enthusiasm to live a more contemplative way of life. Then comes the rude awakening that the fulfillment of our high hopes is, perhaps, going to take considerably longer than we imagined. Discovering within ourselves the tenacious nature of forgetfulness, we are forced to revise our understanding of the journey ahead as being not a short hop into enlightenment, but rather a lifelong process of compassionately working through our deep-seated tendencies to forget again and again the divinity to which we are again and again awakened. You know what it is like, as I do: The all too familiar pattern of being awakened to the depths only to become forgetful of the depths, only to become once again awakened, only to drift off into the nether regions of egocentric living.

Such is the nature of our enlightened ignorance, the painful dance of ecstasy and indifference in which we experience our impotency to make effective our choice to be who we, in our moments of contemplative awakening, intimately know ourselves to be. It is out of all this messy stuff, deeply tasted, deeply accepted, that we are awakened to love stirring in the dark depths of our dilemma—a compassionate love that recognizes and goes forth to identify with the preciousness of all who are lost in ignorance and in the suffering ignorance spawns.

In our enlightened ignorance, we humbly acknowledge that we are among those lost in ignorance. As seen through the eyes of compassionate love, however, we learn not to perpetuate violence toward ourselves in our fragility, but rather to recognize and go forth to identify with the preciousness of ourselves in our fragility. This interior movement of compassionate love is at the heart of our meditation practice, for as seen through the eyes of compassionate love each distraction that arises in meditation is love's opportunity to go forth, to find and fetch back the preciousness of ourselves subject to straying from the present moment. On a broader scale, as seen through the eyes of compassionate love, we see how each personal failing, each personal shortcoming is love's opportunity for us to find and identify with the invincible preciousness of ourselves still subject to the forces of ignorance.

When seen through the eyes of compassionate love this third instance of our contemplative self-transformation can be likened to climbing stairs. The leg that has ascended to the higher stair lifts up the leg that is still on the stair below, which, in the momentum of the lifting, goes up to the still higher stair, so as in turn to lift up the leg that is now below it. Similarly, the part of us that is more enlightened, more awake, more grounded in the divinity of the present moment compassionately recognizes the preciousness of the part of us that is less enlightened, less awake, less grounded and in this loving recognition lifts it up so that by compassionate love we might become one and whole in the love in which we make our ascent.

If we were not enlightened in any sense whatsoever there would be no inner impetus for the journey, for we would be entirely unaware that there was any journey to make. If we were entirely enlightened there would be no journey yet to make, for we would be entirely at home in the full awareness of the godly nature of the present moment. But in the journey there is the part of us that is more enlightened, moving forward, not by leaving behind the part of us that is lost in ignorance, but rather by lovingly recognizing, identifying with, and lifting up the preciousness of ourselves still subject to the forces of ignorance. We make our ascent not by ascending beyond the reach of our brokenness, but rather by a perpetual yielding to a compassionate love that impels us to wait for, go back for, and identify with the preciousness of that in us that still lags behind in varying degrees of ignorance and suffering.

A great paradox about contemplative living, one which never quite ceases to amaze us, is how in humbly embracing with loving compassion that in us which is most lost and broken, the seemingly far off goal of our self-transformation into God begins to shine through the transparency of our humble embrace. Our compassion for ourselves in our brokenness, while truly our own, is contemplatively realized to be not simply our own, but rather the compassionate presence of God manifesting itself in and as our compassion for ourselves.

Grace amazes us, not by resolving the riddle of our forgetfulness, but by dissolving it in a love that lays bare the preciousness of ourselves in our forgetfulness. And in this way, our ignorance, deeply experienced, deeply accepted, proves to be the place where love works most freely in disclosing that our very estrangement from the divine is wholly permeated with the divine.

A fourth instance or aspect of finding and entering our contemplative community is the interpersonal dimension of being in the presence of someone with whom we realize we are not alone on the often lonely path of contemplative self-transformation. Perhaps this person is your own wife or husband. Lucky you, to live with the one, who by his or her very presence, continues to awaken and encourage your attentiveness to the call to be the contemplative person that you deep down really are and are called to be. Perhaps this person is a close friend, one with whom you get together to be encouraged and guided in the path, simply by being in each other's presence and by sharing with one another whatever each of you feels moved to share. Lucky you, to have such a friend whose very presence gives witness that you are not alone on the path of learning to yield to the divinity of daily living.

Perhaps you have such a friend, but he or she has long since moved to some far off place. This can be difficult, especially at first. But no matter, for the essentially dimensionless mystery the friendship embodies is such that geography has no power over it. Perhaps you have such a spouse or such a friend, but he or she has died. This is difficult, especially at first. But no matter, for the essentially deathless mystery the relationship embodies is such that death has no power over it.

As the years go by, as events continue to expand out into an ever wider range, we discover ourselves to be in a living fabric of such relationships that we intimately know live on forever. People once close remain close though now living far away. People once close remain close though now dead. Here is an intimate finding of contemplative community, consisting of an intimate tasting of an ineffable communion with others with whom and through whom the mystery we seek has and continues to manifest itself.

Sometimes this fourth, interpersonal instance of finding and entering one's contemplative community arises in situations in which we are present in the audience, where a poet, an artist, a lover of God, a mystic, a disciple of Jesus, a Buddhist master, or one aflame with a commitment to help the poor holds forth the mystery, rips it open, lets it all pour out. It is not the ego of the graced person around whom all are gathered, but rather the graced person's childlike fidelity and transparency to the mystery that comes welling up and out, uniting all who are present in a communal moment of contemplative wakefulness.

I once heard the pianist Arthur Rubinstein being interviewed. At one point in the interview he was asked to share his experience of playing Chopin's Nocturnes. I do not recall his exact words, but he said in effect, "I do not know what it is. But over and over again I have had the experience of sitting in a crowded concert hall playing the Nocturnes and I can feel everyone in the room waiting for the next note." The moment in which all present, including Rubinstein, wait for the next note, is the moment in which all present find their contemplative community in their oneness with one another in the boundless mystery that enraptures them.

Sometimes this collective experience of contemplative wakefulness is elicited not by an intimate companion or the presence of gifted person, but rather by an event inherently endowed with a meaning and rhythmic power that evokes a communal contemplative experience uniting all who are present. Liturgy is such a gathering, at least this is the potential liturgy has when it is carried out in a committed and prayerful manner. A silent retreat is also such a gathering. When I give or attend silent retreats I am often struck by the extent to which the grace of the retreat is found in this communal dimension of the retreat experience. In fact, one of the most frequently expressed sentiments I hear during these retreats is how good it is simply to be in a room filled with people who are present, each in his or her own way, out of a simple, childlike desire to live a more contemplative way of life.

Events such as liturgy and retreats are continuous with the instinctive movement toward forming a more established, ongoing experience of contemplative community, in which seekers gather to draw from one another encouragement and guidance in contemplative living. In the Buddhist tradition the contemplative community is called the *sangha*. The seeker takes refuge in the *sangha* as a path of self-transformation. In our own Christian tradition the impetus toward contemplative community historically gave rise to the great monastic and religious orders of the church. And today, this same impetus toward contemplative community is expressing itself in a movement in which Christians are gathering in small groups to practice meditation and contemplative prayer.

The communal life of any contemplative gathering is most singularly experienced and expressed in the communal stillness in which all present sit together in meditation. The Zen master Teish Eisho has observed that one log burning in a fireplace does not burn as easily and as intensely as several logs burning together. For when several logs are burning together each log contributes to and draws from the collective flame that unites all the logs as one.[6] Meditating with others, Teish Eisho observes, is like this. Each one present draws from and contributes to a collective presence that embodies and gives witness to the Presence in which all sit as one.

The wordless, communal experience of meditating together spreads out and diffuses itself through all the group experiences in simply being together. Sometimes this being together is expressed in the community's collective commitment to a project, such as collecting food or clothing for the poor, or preparing for a retreat or conference. Sometimes the communal grace of the community is expressed and experienced in the group's compassionate love for and acceptance of its more colorful and not necessarily so easy to deal with members. In these and in other ways a contemplative community experiences and gives witness to the unitive nature of the mystery each member has, to some degree, realized and, in his or her ongoing participation in the community, seeks to realize more fully.

When I am about to start a silent retreat or when I sit waiting to begin the monthly gathering of the contemplative prayer community at my local parish I watch the people filing into the room. I sit aware that I and each one entering the room has been drawn to this place by the instances of contemplative community which have been poetically touched upon in this chapter. That is to say, each one coming into the room is a living embodiment of the unitive nature of reality to which he or she has been awakened in an intimate, intuitive, body-grounded way. Each one entering the room is at the cutting edge of a grace engendering a riddle, which, in being entered into and embraced, is in turn giving rise to new graces. Each is coming in to hear a little talk about contemplative self-transformation and to sit in meditation, during which he or she will draw from and contribute to the communal stillness of the practice. In that stillness each will, hopefully, taste something of the communal mystery in which we are precious and whole in our fragmentation. God inhales, drawing us into places where we gather together in the hope of tasting yet once again the communal mystery that is our life. And God exhales, sending all of us back out into the day by day circumstances in which we are to discover the communal mystery of God, one with us, one with others, one with the earth that sustains us. It is this dimension of contemplative community realized in the concrete immediacy of everyday living that we will continue to explore in the next chapter.

7. The Developmental Revelations of Contemplative Community

In this chapter we will continue to explore the process of finding and entering our contemplative community. As before, our emphasis will not be on finding and entering our contemplative community in the narrow sense of finding a group of people who share with us a desire to live a more contemplative way of life. Rather, our emphasis will continue to be on finding and entering our contemplative community in the more fundamental sense of contemplative experience itself awakening us to the unitive nature of the life we are living. The previous chapter progressed by way of exploring the various instances or aspects of contemplative experience. This chapter will progress by way of exploring moments of childhood development, viewed as contemplative moments in which we are first awakened to ongoing dimensions of our essential being, one with God, one with others, with the earth that sustains us.

We are born as infants, one with the living fabric of birth, breath, milk, and growth. As our eyes begin to focus, there is for us that first moment in which the hazy moon of our mother's face first comes into view, embodying our first vision of the earth as a welcoming place of shapes and forms. In the beginning, we experience ourselves to be continuous with the world that welcomes us. At first, our awareness is submerged in an oceanic bodily vitality of sensory experience. In the beginning, there is, as yet, no sense of self distinguishable from our bodily experiences, which are in turn, indistinguishable from the earth, transparently embodied in our mother's breast, in her milk, and in the calming effects of a blanket which she wraps around us to keep us warm.

In this pre-ego level of consciousness of early infancy, we are first awakened to the transpersonal contemplative community of our oneness with the divinity of the earth and the fabric of all living things. With our first experience as infants, one with the earth, inscribed in our being, it is not surprising that we, as adults, find that when we are in the midst of nature, we are so readily awakened to the nearness of our origin, with all its ineffable wonder, its intimations of the divine.

The power of nature to evoke the contemplative experience of our oneness with the world continues to occur throughout our lives in something as simple and fundamental as cresting a hill overlooking an expansive view. It is as if in reaching the crest of the hill, the one who is first to arrive is the child-self, ageless and wise, who instantaneously sees in the expanse of earth and sky a timeless mystery in which it finds its delight. By the time the part of us that obsesses over the meaning of it all arrives a split second later, carrying on its back all its tomes and notes, huffing and puffing from the ascent, the child-self is already playing in the unity it so spontaneously beholds and which, in its playful wonder, it so exquisitely expresses.

In sharing this metaphor of the ascent, I have in mind my own experience of the first time I saw the Grand Canyon. I remember standing there, observing now this rock formation, now that distant configuration of cliffs with its hint of configurations beyond. All sorts of questions came to me concerning the geological processes in which the canyon first came into existence and under the influences of which it was still being formed. I recall wondering about what kind of mineral deposits made up the rich array of colors and what Indian tribe once, and perhaps still, knew as their home this view I was now beholding. I recall, too, coming up with my own tentative answers to my own questions and resolving that I would find books containing information about these matters.

All these observations with their attendant questions have become somewhat vague to me over the years. But what remains within me, fresh and new and untouched by time, is that awe-filled instant of first coming to the brink—that first instant of being suddenly awakened to and lost in an awareness of myself one with . . . with what? I could not say. Nor can I say to this day. In the awe-filled instant of which I now speak, the part of me that asks and answers questions had not yet arrived on the scene. There was in this timeless moment but a body-grounded awakening to an awe-evoking presence, with which I was and am unthinkably, unquestionably one.

The contemplative experience of the divinity of our oneness with nature, to which we are first awakened in our infancy, continues to flow through our childhood years. We grow up getting our bearings in the universe by internalizing the geography of a pattern formed by a certain tree outside our kitchen window, a large rock embedded in a hillside, a bend in the bay, a bit of sparse grass between two buildings. If, as we grow older we have to leave our home for an extended period of time, like, for instance, the rest of our life, we take this internalized geography along with us. We leave, knowing that we might one day return to visit this place in which we first awakened to the graced mystery of being in a place.

If, perhaps, years later, we actually do return to visit the place we first called home, something in us is careful to note whether the things of the earth we first knew as a child are still there. If they are still there we are strangely and subtly reassured. If they are not, we feel the loss of the internalized geography of our childhood no longer having its corresponding external counterpart. If, for example, while out walking, we are surprised to discover that the stand of willows in which we played as a child is no longer there, we silently say to ourselves, "I wonder what became of the willows that used to stand over there?" In the asking we can see the willows in our mind's eye, and see our child-self running through their arched hallways of shadow and light in which, along with our friends, we came upon secret things, not for the telling.

Thomas Merton writes of sitting alone in the woods when suddenly "the silence was broken by the song of a bird announcing the difference between heaven and hell." A bird, as far as we know, is not empowered to know the difference between heaven and hell that its song proclaims. But we are. We know, all too well, the hell of going about unaware of, and unresponsive to, the divinity of the life we are living. And we know the fleeting glimpse of heaven granted in being lulled into awareness by something as simple as a single leaf or stone, or in being jolted into awareness by something as dramatic as unexpectedly coming upon a deer, head full of antlers, eyes full of God.

Here is a meditation practice you can try. Or perhaps simply reading about it will prove helpful in clarifying the potential contemplative practices have in awakening us to the divinity manifested in our oneness with the world of nature. Go to your room about an hour before sunset. Prop a few pillows on the floor against a wall facing an open window. Sit on the floor. Do not read anything. Do not write anything. But simply settle into the single-minded intention of being with God while it gets dark. Continue sitting silent and still in the slowly darkening room for a full hour or so once the room has become dark. If you sit with any intention other than that of simply being with God in the deepening darkness of day's end you may or may not succeed. Sitting with the intention of simply staying awake, you might fall asleep. Sitting with the intention of falling asleep, you might have insomnia and sit there wide awake. Sitting with the intention of finding inner peace, you may be agitated. Sitting with the intention of having certain religious experiences you might find yourself bereft of any felt sense of God's presence. But if you sit there in the darkening room with no intention save that of being with God while it gets dark, you will succeed without fail, no matter what.

For you have been with God every night since those first nights in which, as an infant, you drifted off to sleep, held by your mother in a darkening room. This is so insofar as being with God while it gets dark is understood as a metaphor giving witness to the contemplative experience of day's end manifesting the unmanifested mystery of God. Such an understanding comes not with thinking, but with yielding to the all encompassing nature of day's end, yielding, without pretense, to the sheer immediacy of the immensity of night.

Sitting with all one's heart in a darkening room seems strange only to the extent that you have allowed yourself to become a stranger to this childlike vulnerability to the divinity of day's end. Becoming a stranger to the divinity of day's end is, unfortunately, all too easy to do: You come home at night drained by the day's ventures, ruminating over what tomorrow might bring, distracting yourself with this or that diversion, then get into bed, slipping off to sleep without ever stopping to renew your mindfulness of the divinity of day's end.

It is in this enlightened ignorance of knowing by experience how easy it is to be unaware of the divinity of life that you are interiorly drawn to this moment in which you now sit, sincerely intent on being with God while it gets dark. Sitting silent and still, you allow yourself to fall out of the overarching mesh of thoughts and concerns that tend to preoccupy you during most of your waking hours. You sit, allowing yourself to fall down into the eternal silence of the darkening room, where the shadowy array of things silently radiate a never-to-be exhausted fullness. You sit, empty of concerns and goals, utterly given over to an intimate awareness of your unthinkable oneness with the fullness of the night.

At first, your ego fights the descent into the divinity of night, struggles with time spent with no agenda, no goals save this unmanageable situation of nothing to manage, nothing to control. Little by little, however, as your ego melts into the darkness, you discover yourself to be resting in and one with the no-place-to-go plenitude of the darkened room in which you sit. Sitting thus, for an hour or so in the darkness, trusting the felt sense of when to slowly stand, you stand and, without turning on any lights, undress in the dark. Getting into bed, you drift off to sleep as one graced in having been intimately awakened and surrendered over to the divinity of night. Not a bad way to end a day.

In the gospels we read of how Jesus saw and invited us to see in a mustard seed, a fig tree, the birds of the air, the flowers of the field, a storm at sea, some bread and wine—manifestations of God's loving nearness. In the long and rich heritage of the contemplative traditions we read of Saint Francis of Assisi calling the sun his brother and the moon his sister, and Saint John of the Cross proclaiming, "my beloved is the mountains." These are but a few of the numerous examples that could be cited in which scripture and the contemplative traditions invite us to trust in what our own heart knows to be true—that our oneness with God is manifested in our contemplatively realized oneness with the divinity of the earth, with the fabric of all living things.

All this is said as an invitation to realize that we have already found our contemplatively realized oneness with the divinity of the earth in our infancy, and in each instance in which we have been ineffably awakened to our ineffable oneness with the ineffable mystery nature manifests. In realizing that we have found our contemplative oneness with the divinity of the earth, we can then with greater clarity, choose to enter into this oneness by the way we live. We can drink water and bathe as contemplative practices, which is to say, as a ways of renewing our awareness of our oneness with the primordial givenness of water of which our bodies are primarily composed. We can prepare and eat our meals as a contemplative practice, embodying a visceral awareness of the eucharistic nature of every meal. We can practice meditation in which we can experience for ourselves how sitting absorbed in bare attention of the primordial, life-giving rhythms of our breathing, lays bare the mystery to which we were first awakened in our infancy. We can take walks as a contemplative practice, in which we can learn to sense with each footfall, the presence of God, manifested in and as the earth on which we are walking, on which we are all living out our lives, and in which, at death, we come to rest. We can allow these and similar practices to establish us in a spirituality of the ecology, in which we come to recognize, honor and give witness to the divinity manifested in our oneness with the earth and with the fabric of all living things.

The diffused, global awareness of our oneness with the earth to which we are first awakened in infancy evolves into our first *personal* awakening of ourselves as distinct from yet one with others. This first dawning of personal awareness comes to us in that moment when the hazy moon of our mother's face first comes into

view, not simply as a point of encounter with our oneness with primordial roundness, with earthly shape and
form, but, what is more, as a point of encounter with
our own, newly emerging personal presence, distinct
from yet one with the personal presence of our
mother.[1] Gazing into her eyes as she gazes into ours,
alone together, we are, each to each, not one, not two.
That is to say, in this moment of contemplative communion each is to the other a witness of the other's otherness. The mother holds not herself, but one
delightfully other than herself. And the infant is held by
one who is not itself, but rather the one in whose presence its own unique presence is now emerging. All this
emerging awareness of otherness goes on in the context
of a sustained communion, in which the mother holds
one who, though not herself is, nonetheless, not wholly
or simply other than herself. So, too, the infant is held
by one who, though not itself, is, nonetheless, not
wholly or simply other than itself. In the midst of their
otherness, they are in the midst of their oneness. It is in
this not-one, not-two, ineffable communion that personal presence first awakens.

As a child grows older, the not-one, not-two quality
of personal awareness evolves to the point that it can
begin to express this awareness in its first personal
responses to its parents' personal presence. The contemplatively sensed importance of the infant personally
responding to its parents' personal presence is revealed
in the zeal with which parents attempt to evoke their
child's first smile. Making faces, making sounds, looking
into the infant's eyes, they keep cajoling, keep waiting
for the infant to smile back. Love keeps prompting them
to continue in their efforts in which love flows through
them into the child, where it wells up, finally spilling
over in the first moment the infant smiles back. This
moment of love returning to itself evokes a timeless joy
in which our ultimate identity and destiny is revealed.

Imagine a small child who wants a particular present very much for Christmas, but who thinks the present is too much to hope for. Imagine, too, that the child's mother gets the present. On Christmas morning, as her child is opening the package containing the present too good to hope for, the mother can barely wait for the moment the lid comes off the box. And when the moment finally comes in which the child's face lights up in realizing the present too good to hope for has been given, the mother is not there. That is to say, she is not sitting there dualistically observing herself observe her child. Rather, she so delights in the child's delight that she is lost in the child's face. Love does it to her. Yet, afterwards, in looking back at this moment, she does not count this love induced loss of self-reflective awareness as loss but as pure gain. It is as if in this moment a curtain fleetingly opened and she was allowed to glimpse what in her heart she knows is always true—only love, and all that is given in love, is ultimately real. Love alone has the power to reveal and to fulfill who we deep down really are and are called to be.

Taking this intimate and universal moment between mother and child to be revelatory of God's never ending oneness with us, we can suggest a poetic vision in which our life is seen as God's gift to us. The gift comes wrapped in our own unforeseeable future, which is unwrapped in living out all our days. Our death is the moment God can barely wait for, knowing it to be the moment we, finally becoming all unwrapped, will see for ourselves the gift that our life consists of. When the moment of our death finally comes, and we see for our-selves the gift God gave us in giving us our life we are awed beyond belief, for in that moment we discover that we, from the beginning, were given very God! Looking up into the face of God we discover God is not there. God is lost in our face lost in her.

To say that God is lost in our face poetically alludes to the infinite *kenosis* of God, wholly poured out in and as who we simply are as manifestations of the unmanifested mystery of God. To say that the moment of death itself is a realization of the Godly nature of our very life poetically alludes to death as the moment in which an infinite outpouring of love returns to itself in an ecstatic communion that we can but scarcely begin to imagine.

Such imagery invites us to realize that we have already found our contemplative community in our own childhood experiences of interpersonal communion with our parents, and, later on with our friends, and still later on perhaps with our own spouse and children, in short with all those we love and with whom we share our life. We can all look back to these moments of loving communion with others, and sense the importance of trusting in the unending nature of the not-one, not-two communion with one another that such moments reveal. The more consciously we ground ourselves in this awareness, the more we can freely choose to enter into this contemplatively realized community by the way we live.

We can choose to allow our awareness of ourselves as *distinct from others*, to which we were first awakened in our mother's arms, to continue to deepen and expand in an ongoing process of accepting and yielding to our own solitary uniqueness not patterned on the expectations of others. We can spend time alone in silence. We can meditate, and in other ways follow our own inimitable aloneness to its origin, to discover that origin to be God manifested in and as the utterly unique self that we are and are called to be.

We can choose to allow our own sense of *oneness with others*, to which we were first awakened in our mother's arms, to continue to deepen and expand in an ongoing process of loving intimacy and concern for others. Beginning in our own home, neighborhood, and community settings, we can choose the contemplative path of yielding to love's self-transforming ways, by risking to be more present, more real, honest, and vulnerable with those who share their lives with us. We can choose to allow this circle of loving concern to expand out to embrace everyone everywhere, particularly those who suffer and are in need. We can allow ourselves to be so transformed by all that love asks us, as to allow love to carry us to its origin, discovering its origin to be God manifested in and as our genuine, Christ-like love for one another.

As we simultaneously enter into the solitary and communal aspects of our life, we enter into the not-one, not-two nature of the contemplatively realized real world in which solitude and communion keep turning into each other. Entering ever more deeply to our oneness with others, we come to discover the ultimately incommunicable, solitary mystery of our own unfolding life. Entering ever more deeply into our own solitude, we discover the essentially communal nature of our life, one with God, one with others, one with all that is and is not.

The next aspect of the parent-child bond in which we can see revealed the communal dimensions of our essential being appears in the ways in which parents discipline their small children. Small children make mistakes. They spill things, break things, get into things, and sometimes act in ways that are potentially or actually harmful to themselves, their siblings, and their friends. The manner in which the parents correct their small children is critical to the child's well being. If all goes well, the stress and unpleasantness that both child and parents feel in such moments remains established in an underlying tone of compassionate love that carries with it the saving message: "We all make mistakes. We all have our bad moments. You just had one of yours. But nothing you could ever do could ever lessen how much we love you, for you are precious to us in ways that are much bigger than the ups and downs of the daily stuff we all go through."

Even as the parents speak this saving message, they can feel in their bodies the essential, life-giving truth their words convey. The child, too, experiences in her body a sense of relief in the tone of the parent's voice, conveying the reassuring message that the "bad" thing she did does not make her a bad person who is unlovable in some unfixable and irreversible way. If all goes well, this scene of compassionate love repeated over and over, makes the house in which the family lives a home. For home is a place where all are loved and accepted as precious in their collective frailties and mishaps. Breathing in this compassionate atmosphere day by day, a child learns to internalize an unquestioned, simply given sense of herself as precious and lovable in the midst of her ongoing foibles and mishaps.

In real life, however, imperfect parents sometimes encounter their imperfect children in ways that do not convey the healing message of compassionate love but rather a crippling message of shame. The issue here is that as small children we cannot give ourselves the experience of our own preciousness, but must discover our preciousness mirrored in our parents' eyes. And to varying degrees our parents, in their own woundedness, may have failed to mirror back to us our inherent preciousness. Perhaps their failure to love us in the ways we needed to be loved was tragically abusive. Perhaps their failures were more subtle in being essentially loving and well intentioned parents who, in certain moments, conveyed the message that we were lovable only to the extent that we measured up to their expectations. Or the crippling message may have been that we were lovable as long as we did not let them see certain behaviors, weaknesses, and fears within ourselves they did not want to see. Perhaps in our own situation it was not our parents but a dominating older sibling, a teacher, or classmates at school that first instilled the destructive message. Whatever the specifics might be, the root issue is that, to varying degrees, we are subject to carrying within ourselves destructive fears and beliefs that our inadequacies make us an inadequate person. The bad things we sometimes do make us a bad person. Or some particularly secret personal failing must be hidden from ourselves and others in the fear that in being found out we will be exposed as one that no one, including ourselves, would want to be around.

If this shame-based stance toward ourselves is not recognized and healed by compassionate love, our spiritual endeavors can become themselves shame-based attempts to establish as much distance as possible between ourselves and our own frailty and shortcomings. The seemingly lofty and holy self we imagine we are becoming feels secure in making an ascent that leaves far behind the fragile, childlike self that can barely walk on level ground, much less scale the steep inclines of spiritual perfection which we are seeking to master.

Imagine that you have the following dream: You are climbing a high mountain. In the dream you know that the valley below is the place where you grew up and in which you experienced painful things and made all sorts of mistakes. It is this valley of painful memories and self-doubt that you are now trying to transcend and leave behind by reaching the summit on which you will be sublimely holy and one with God. Suddenly, the summit comes into view, and in that same instant the wind, coming up from the valley below, brings with it the sound of a child crying out in distress. Just as suddenly you realize there is no real choice but to renounce the hard fought goal of reaching the summit to go back down the mountain to find and help the hurting child.

Turning back, you descend down into the valley. Following the child's cries as your guide, you are amazed to discover that you have been led (just as, deeper down, you knew you would be) to the home you tried to leave behind in setting out to make your ascent to holiness! Sensing the ungraspable and momentous nature of the moment, you gently open the door and look inside. Sitting there, perhaps in a corner on the floor, is your own wounded child-self—that part of yourself that holds the feelings of powerlessness and shame that you tried so hard to leave behind. Respectfully approaching this hurting child, you sit next to it on the floor. Perhaps for a long time you say nothing, but simply sit there, grateful that you finally had the common sense to come back to this precious enigma of your own wounded child-self. Then a most amazing thing happens. You suddenly realize you are on the lofty summit of union with God! Suddenly, the Christ-event of God going forth to identify with the preciousness of us in our brokenness is realized in and as your compassionate love for the preciousness of yourself in your brokenness.

The dream embodies the power of compassion to reveal to us that we cannot move forward by leaving any part of ourselves behind. We can only move forward in our willingness to go back, to wait forever if need be, until each aspect of ourselves finally awakens to and accepts the divinity of its weakness. Thus, by way of compassionate love, we move ever higher in our willingness to descend ever lower in a perpetual willingness to find, accept, and identify with the preciousness of the weak and childlike aspects of ourselves.

Learning by our own experience that this is true, we begin to appreciate how we have found our contemplative community in our moments of being compassionately loved by ourselves and others in the midst of our frailty. And in this realization we can then choose to enter into this community by the way we live. We can choose to cultivate a sustained stance of compassionate love for ourselves as precious in all our lofty littleness and frailty. This stance of compassionate love for ourselves remains, of course, incomplete unless it spills over into a compassionate love for others as precious in their frailty which is one with ours. By cultivating a daily contemplative stance of compassionate love for self and others, we enter ever more deeply into the contemplative community compassion reveals.

In adolescence and young adulthood the parent-child relationship expands and undergoes yet further transformations disclosing ongoing dimensions of the communal nature of our essential being. The parable of the prodigal son (Lk 15:11-32) graphically portrays the compassionate love dimension of the adolescent and young adult phase of the parent child relationship. We all know the story of the man with two sons. One stayed home. The other deeply grieved his father, foolishly risking his own safety and well being by going to far off places to squander his share of his father's money.

In the days that followed his son's departure we can imagine how the father might have dreamed dreams expressive of his deep longing for his son's return. Perhaps he dreamed of himself searching for his son in dark and unknown places, or of his own heart flowing out in long ribbons of grief into a churning river, and then of himself, strangely down stream gathering up out of the waters all that flowed away. Or we can imagine how the father might have gazed, more times than he could count, at the empty horizon over which his son had disappeared from view. And we can imagine, too, that ecstatic moment in which he glanced up to see the empty horizon filled from end to end with the small speck of his son returning home. Suddenly, the father finds himself running open-armed down the road, knowing, in that instant, no joy save that of an ever narrowing distance between himself and the precious presence of the one who was lost and suffering.

And we can imagine the son in this moment, still walking, his head bent downward, all caught up in rehearsing his lines about hopefully being allowed to be a servant in his father's house. Absorbed in preparing himself as best he could for the moment he would first see his father, he was not prepared (are we ever?) for the moment he first looked up to see, embodied in his father's open-armed advance, the immanent dismantling of all his strategies of servanthood.

Then comes the moment of their encounter: the father, embracing his son as a preciousness almost too precious to bear; the son, at once undone and restored to wholeness in the flurry of embraces received and given. The two of them stand there together out on the open road, each laughing and crying at once, each the cause of losing their balance as each holds the other up in an awkward dance, and our own heart immediately recognizes it as the dance we long to dance. For we all intuit the taste of heaven in the embrace of one once lost returning home.

As we go through life we continue to move in and out of each role depicted in this family saga. Sometimes we are the wayward son. In those moments we find ourselves grateful for the loving presence of one letting us know we remain invincibly precious in the midst of our wayward ways. Sometimes we are the father. In those moments love impels us to see, and go forth to identify with the invincible preciousness of ourselves and others in our collective frailty. And sometimes, all too often in fact, we neither give nor receive compassionate love, but, like the son who stayed at home keeping all the rules, we remain pretty clueless as to what compassionate love is all about.

We are not always compassionate toward ourselves and others. When we are not compassionate, we suffer. When we are compassionate, our suffering is not taken away but is transformed in an ever deeper realization of our communion with each other as precious in our collective frailty. More than this, in the contemplative event of compassion, we realize the presence of God manifested in and as our compassionate love for each other. This, in fact, is the religious dimension of the parable as told by Jesus. In the father, prodigal with love, we are to recognize the manifestation of God, eternally prodigal with love for us in the midst of all the hurtful and foolish things we do to ourselves and others.

Here then is a way of finding and entering our contemplative community that lies open to us all. First, we can pause to remember our own moments of compassionate love given and received. We can remember how, in those moments, all feelings of guilt, shame, and worthlessness suddenly gave way, like a floor in a burning building, leaving us, with no footing in anything whatsoever, save the love into which we were falling. To have known, even for an instant, the joy of such an encounter is to know the abyss-like communion of love in which wayward lives are invincibly established. A moment of compassionate love is essentially a contemplative moment granting an intimate, intuitive, body-grounded awareness of the way we deep down really are, one with the way the one unending present moment really is.

Setting out to enter into the contemplatively realized community that compassionate love discloses will result in frustration if we expect to succeed in living up to some hoped for ideal of becoming, in word and action, the compassionate person we know deep down we really are and are called to be. But, fortunately for us, our progress on the path of compassionate living is not measured primarily in terms of learning never to fail in our efforts to be compassionate. Rather, we move along the path in the self-transforming realization that each failure in compassion is, in essence, an opportunity to be compassionate towards ourselves as invincibly precious and lovable even in our failure to be compassionate. Approached in this way, the path forward consists of discovering again and again that our lives are invincibly established in a wholeness that reigns supreme in the midst of our unruly and wayward ways. Silenced and dumbfounded by the way compassionate love makes our failure to progress the very stuff out of which we progress, we move along the path of our self-transformation. Moving thus, we no longer recognize ourselves and others according to the old markers of progress and attainment. For our very notion of progress and attainment have become themselves transformed in the gratitude and humility that arises each time compassionate love is given and received.

There is a humble, down-to-earth way that we can cultivate finding and entering our contemplative community along the lines being indicated here. This way consists of first entering as best we can into a contemplatively realized communal oneness with our own fundamental needs and the simply given life these needs reveal. Feeling hungry, we can prepare a meal and eat, mindful of the simply given nature of hunger, food, and eating. Feeling tired, we can lie down to rest, mindful of the simply given nature of fatigue and rest. Feeling lonely, we can be alone, mindful of the simply given nature of our aloneness and the mysterious sense of oneness with God, the earth, and others that we, at times, experience in it. In being intimate with another person we can be mindful of the simply given, never-ending fulfillment that intimacy reveals.

As we enter into this path of a humble and grateful recognition and acceptance of our God given needs, we catch ourselves in the act of neglecting or abusing the simply given life these needs manifest. We might, for example, discover more consciously than ever before how basic needs such as getting enough sleep and exercise, maintaining a proper diet, relaxing with friends and family, taking time to read a good book, not to mention being faithful to times of meditation and prayer are being compromised. In fact, we may have to admit that such basic needs are being compromised to the point of presenting real threats to our health and well being. What is more, we might discover how we, in seeing the ingrained patterns of self-neglect and abuse, tend to heap self-shaming messages on ourselves in that inner voice that scolds and condemns us for "being the way we are."

As we become more astute in humble self-knowledge, we might discover that attitudes and patterns of behavior that we have tended to interpret as being self-indulgent are, in actual fact, addictive patterns of neglecting and abusing deeper, more foundational aspects our selves. We might come to see, for example, that a pattern of compulsive sexual activity is masking the fear of risking real intimacy. Addictive eating is masking unmet needs for nourishment. Work addiction is masking and perpetuating an ongoing neglect of the need to be genuinely grounded and present in the workplace.

The relevance of these and similar patterns of self-neglect and abuse to our present reflections is enhanced by the fact that these self-limiting patterns sometimes prove to be internalized patterns of parental neglect and abuse. For we are made in such a way that moments in which our parents, in their own woundedness, wounded us by their neglectful or abusive behavior becomes internalized as ritualized patterns in which we continue to abuse and neglect ourselves. A child who is screamed at or hit is likely to grow up with internalized patterns of either excessive passivity and compliance or a propensity to episodes of intense rage. A child who is a victim of incest is likely to grow up with internalized patterns of either repressed sexuality or sexually compulsive behavior. A child who grows up in a house where food is offered in lieu of love is likely to grow up with unhealthy and compulsive eating patterns. A child who grows up with the message from its parents that it is loved and lovable only to the extent it measures up to its parents' expectations, is likely to grow up subject to narcissistic perfectionism in which it seeks to be loved by winning the recognition and admiration of others.

As we look, in an honest and humble fashion, into our own unique version of the universal story of human suffering, we can see the extent to which we might be using our spirituality as a means of putting as much distance as possible between our conscious experience of ourselves and those aspects of ourselves that we are trying to conquer or leave behind. The externals of this distancing process take many forms, ranging from faith in Christ, faith in the church, committing ourselves to social justice, striving in deep meditation to reach enlightenment or contemplative intimacy with God. But regardless of how the externals may vary, the root issue remains the same: as long as our religious faith and spirituality are being used as a means of distancing ourselves from our own unacknowledged, undealt with brokenness, our spirituality and religious faith will tend to add to instead of deliver us from our difficulties.

When religious faith and spirituality are used in this way, they perpetuate the suffering that inevitably follows upon wanting life to be other than it is. Life is such that we must love our neighbor *as* and not instead of ourselves. We cannot genuinely love God and serve others while at the same time continuing to deny, neglect, or despise any aspect of ourselves. Deprivation of our own real needs breeds not generosity but fear-based possessiveness, irritability, and feigned forms of concern for others. The mask eventually wears thin and breaks open. We cannot with impunity abandon or perpetuate abuse on ourselves under the guise of being committed to lofty spiritual ideals. We cannot cheat the axioms of compassionate love inscribed in our very being and hope to live any kind of spiritual life that is real and life-giving.

Finding and entering our contemplative community by way of committing ourselves to a path of compassionate love begins in humbly asking God for the grace to recognize and go forth to identify with the preciousness of ourselves trapped in the ignorance of self-abandonment and neglect. And, in this same loving stance, we can patiently take steps to replace abandonment with nurture, absence with presence, deprivation with prodigal, compassionate love for ourselves as invincibly precious in our fragility.

Of course, this loving honesty and generosity toward ourselves as precious in our brokenness remains incomplete and unfulfilled unless it spills over into genuine engagement with others, one with us as precious in their brokenness. We saw above how this holds true with respect to our collective littleness and frailty. But it is just as true with respect to the more adult ways in which we are all subject to perpetuating violence on ourselves and others. The following personal experience dramatically brought home to me the contemplative community that arises in our compassionate love for one another in our collective propensity to harm ourselves and others.

As part of my doctoral training, I worked at a large hospital on a thirty day inpatient treatment center for alcohol and drug addiction. Early on in the history of this treatment center the patients devised an initiation rite, which, by the time I was there, had become something of an ongoing tradition as part of the process a person had to go through to be admitted to the unit.

The initiation rite was held in a large room on the ward. The fifty or so members of the unit sat with their chairs facing inward around the four walls of the room. The middle of the room around which the members sat was empty of all furniture, except for two chairs in the middle of the room facing each other about four feet apart. The alcoholic seeking admittance onto the unit was led into the room by one of the members of the unit, who instructed him to sit down in one of the two chairs in the middle of the room. As the newcomer was being led into the room and instructed to sit down, the alcoholics seated along the four walls of the room would all be looking downward providing no eye contact, no smiles, no indication to the newcomer of what to expect.

Once the newcomer sat down, the member of the unit presiding at the rite of passage would sit down in the chair across from him, look him straight in the eye and ask, "What do you love the most?" The newcomer, who was, in most cases, fresh in off the streets, still shaky from the effects of severe, life-threatening alcohol abuse, would often blurt out something like "my wife." At which point, the silence of room would be abruptly shattered by the all the men lining the four walls of the room loudly yelling out in unison, "bullshit!" Startled and unnerved, the newcomer would find himself sitting in the collective, serious as death, silence of all the men encircling him, each of them looking downward, offering no point of contact, except their abrupt challenge to his destructive self-deception. The interviewer would then, without delay, repeat the question, "What do you love the most?" The newcomer, this time with some trepidation, would say something like, "My children." At which point the group would once again yell, "bullshit." This would continue, until, the newcomer would finally say, "alcohol." At which point everyone in the room would break into applause. All would stand. The newcomer was instructed to stand. The members of the unit would line up, single file, in complete silence, as each in turn held the newcomer in a genuine embrace, welcoming him into their midst. Sometimes, I would see tears coming to the newcomer's eyes, as tears would come to my own eyes as well. I could sense that this was perhaps the first time this man had been touched, really touched, in a long, long time. This moment of communal compassion did not mark the end of a journey, but rather the beginning of a long one.

This long journey is the one we are all on together, learning to extend to one another the compassionate love that reveals the communal preciousness of ourselves in our communal weakness. Sometimes compassion compels us to confront, sometimes to cajole, sometimes to be silent and wait, sometimes to do or say what it would never occur to our egocentric self to do or say, for we can never say for certain in advance just how compassionate love may prompt us to act. We can never know with certainty up front just what compassionate love may ask us to see, and accept within ourselves and others. But this much is certain, in our willingness to recognize and go forth to identify with the preciousness of ourselves and others in our collective frailty, we discover our contemplative community in the intimate texture of our daily dealings with one another. We discover our contemplative community in the Christ event of God manifested in and as our willingness to love ourselves and others as precious and whole in the midst of our fragmentation.

PART FOUR:

FIND YOUR CONTEMPLATIVE TEACHING
AND FOLLOW IT

8. Discerning That Which Enhances

It is not enough for us simply to commit ourselves to our contemplative practices and the communal dimensions of our daily living and assume that our efforts will bring us to the contemplative way of life we long to realize. What must be dealt with every step of the way is our propensity for self-deception, in which, without even realizing it, we get in our own way by compromising and doing violence to the very process of self-transformation we are attempting to cultivate. Realizing this is so, we instinctively seek out the guiding light of contemplative wisdom by which we can discern that which enhances from that which hinders the self-transformation we seek to realize.

Contemplative wisdom can come to us through a spiritual director, spiritual reading, our own prayer and meditation, or whatever other source we are fortunate enough to find. The question being raised in this chapter regarding the matter of discernment is this: What is it that contemplative wisdom looks for in order to discern that we are on the path that enhances rather than the path that hinders our ongoing contemplative self-transformation? I answer this way: Contemplative wisdom discerns our efforts in contemplative living to be effective insofar as our efforts are bringing us, without our knowing how, into the horizonless domain of serenity in the no-hope-for-recovery situation. We can discern the effectiveness of our efforts insofar as they embody our stepping across the line to join those who have come to serenity in knowing they are about to die.

Other reference points of discernment could just as effectively be used: birth, falling in love, the artist's ecstasy, prayer, or any other arena of contemplative awakening in which the opaqueness of the egocentric self is rendered transparent to the divinity our daily living manifests. But making death our focus has the advantage of reminding us of the unto-death nature of the life we are living. For, in truth, we are about to die. Breath by breath we are living our one-less-breath-to-breathe life. To step across the line to join those about to die is simply to accept that there is no line to step across, save an imaginary one the ego draws as a way of preserving its illusions about itself as being the sum and substance of who we are and what we are about. This is what makes those who have come to serenity in the face of death to be such a fecund source of contemplative discernment. By their humble acceptance of their lot, they reveal the illusory nature of the ego's be-all and end-all posturing. As all that is tangible dissolves away, their serenity gives witness to a body-grounded awareness of a mystery that precedes, transcends, and wholly permeates the unthinkable nature of life and death.

By using death as our primary reference point in contemplative discernment we must, however, be careful not to romanticize what is quite often a situation entailing incalculable suffering. It is a sacrilege to romanticize suffering, to gloss over it with seemingly spiritual language that avoids meeting and being eye to eye with the one who is suffering. It is a distortion of the truth of things not to admit and allow ourselves to feel the sadness, fear, and other emotions that spring up in the face of death. But it is as well a manifestation of ignorance not to recognize the self-transforming light that shines through the no-hope-for-recovery situation, revealing to us that just because there is no hope for recovery does not mean there is no hope.

The light shining through the no-hope-for-recovery situation is at the heart of Christian faith. If any of us could witness the crucifixion, images of its brutality and violence would no doubt haunt us all our days. And yet, even though the tragedy is real, nightmarish, and unthinkable, we believe as Christians that the cross marks the spot where God reveals the all encompassing emptiness out of which the light of resurrection eternally shines in our hearts. Our faith in the revelatory nature of the death of Jesus reveals to us the true nature of our own death as being our moment of entrance into an undying awareness of our eternal union with God. This truth of faith is expressed in the words Saint Mechtilde heard God speak to her, "Do not fear your death. For when that moment comes I will draw in my breath and your soul will come to me like a needle to a magnet."

It seems then that, although birth, prayer, or some other arena of contemplative self-transformation could be used as our primary reference point in contemplative wisdom, death has the advantage of heightening our understanding of the ultimate radicality of the path of contemplative living. As illumined by death awareness, the ultimate radicality of contemplative living is discovered to be a continual willingness to die to our egocentricity so that we might begin to taste, even on this earth, the bliss of those who, having died, see God "face to face."

It is within the context of considerations such as these that our method of discernment emerges: First, we look upon those who have come to serenity in the face of death as manifesting to us the distilled essence of living in childlike transparency to the ineffable. Then, within the context of this reverential awareness of those

about to die, we tease out some of the salient characteristics of their serenity, so that by finding these same
characteristics within ourselves we can discern we are
on the path that enhances the contemplative way of life
we seek to live.

Our first poetic image of death and dying will be
that of a woman who has become old. Becoming old
does not mean that death is immanent in the sense that
death will necessarily occur this evening, next week, or
even this year or the next. But becoming old means that
death is immanent in that one knows that if the first
seventy or eighty years flew by so quickly, the relatively
little time that is left is passing like a blink. To be at
peace in old age is to be at peace with the nearness of
death, not as some alien force that threatens to snatch
away the gift of life, but rather as a rapidly approaching
point of the journey beyond which only the eyes of
faith and contemplative experience can see.

Imagine a woman who lives alone and who each
morning goes out to work in her garden. She is old. She
knows she is old. But from time to time there in the garden she is given that which makes her growing old
strangely irrelevant, her approaching death strangely
without consequence. It comes over her in the stacking
of clay pots, in seeing the ink-eyed swiftness of chip-
munks darting about the shadows, causing her little girl
inside to smile, even laugh. It comes over her as she
moves like the will-o'-the-wisp in a straw hat over the
narrow brick pathways she herself put down, brick by
brick, many summers ago. It comes over her as she
drops small dry seeds into the waiting earth, knowing
all up and down her living soul the promise each small
dry seed contains.

With this old woman as our intuitive reference
point, we can draw out and bring into focus our first
characteristic of the dying process which we can look
for in ourselves in discerning that we are on the
path that enhances our ongoing contemplative
self-transformation. Those about to die are in water over

their heads. Something very big, something that changes everything completely, has found its way into the there-is-nothing-they-can-do-about-it center of their very existence. So, too, with us. Like those about to die, we, as seekers of the contemplative way, are in water over our heads. We always have been. From conception onwards we are in water over our heads. For who can fathom what it is to be? From before we were conceived we are in water over our heads. For who can fathom what it is not to be? But while this is true of everything and everyone, it is especially true of us as seekers of the contemplative way because we have been intimately awakened to the cannot-get-to-the-bottom-of-it nature of the life we are living.

We can discern we are on the path that enhances when we discern that we are learning what those who are very old have come to learn concerning the fathomless nature of that which simply is. True, we forget that we have been awakened to the depths. We fall back into the ignorance of "obsessing over what we think is the meaning of it all." But this proves to be no hindrance. For the I-cannot-get-to the-bottom-of-it nature of the life we are living is so big as to permeate even our forgetfulness of it, making our very forgetfulness itself a fathomless mystery in which, being accepted with humility and gratitude, we grow all the stronger.

The following Zen *koan* invites us to see directly into the fathomless nature of reality: "A water buffalo passes easily, horns, head, shoulders and all, through a latticed window. What gets stuck is its tail!"[1] When someone is dying that person is the water buffalo passing head, horns, shoulders and all through the latticed window. What gets stuck is the dying person's unfinished business, until it too, being worked through and finally let go of, easily passes through. The whole universe simply arising—whole, complete, and unencumbered in the present moment—is the water buffalo passing through the lattice window. Who we are right now in the immediacy of the present moment before thought begins is the water buffalo passing through the lattice window. What gets stuck is all our still clung-to doubting. What gets stuck is all that we have not yet surrendered over to the in-over-our-heads nature of the one unending present moment in which our lives unfold.

The lovely and profound Buddhist scripture *The Diamond Sutra* consists of a series of dialogues between the Buddha and his disciple Subhuti. With *koan*-like directness, section XXII of this sacred text gives witness to the contemplative wisdom of experiencing directly the ineffable nature of what simply is. The chapter in its entirety reads as follows:

> Then Subhuti asked Buddha: World honored One, in the attainment of the Consummation of Incomparable Enlightenment did Buddha make no acquistion whatsoever?
> Buddha replied: Just so, Subhuti. Through the Consummation of Incomparable Enlightenment I acquired not even the least thing; wherefore it is called "Consummation of Incomparable Enlightenment."[2]

If the Buddha would have acquired anything, his enlightenment would be comparable to another enlightenment in which something else was attained. But in attaining "not even the least thing," the enlightenment is incomparable in having as its content nothing but the incomparable nature of the all encompassing totality the present moment manifests. One who has come to serenity in death attains not even the least thing, and, in this incomparable non-attainment manifests the ineffable oneness of life and death. This then is the first sign of resonance we can look for between ourselves and those who have come to serenity in death—the dawning of an awakening that is very big, which changes everything completely, and in which nothing is attained save a heart awakened to the fathomless nature of reality—the infinity of which we call God.

A second characteristic of those who have come to serenity in facing death is that of coming to a place in which nothing helps and yet in which the smallest of things help. Imagine that you are in your bed at night, that the moment of death is immanent. You are alone in a strange thoughtless clarity. The flowers on the windowsill, silhouetted in the moonlight, seem to know all about it. Nothing helps to bring you back from the edge of the precipice over which you have already begun to make your descent. And yet, though nothing helps, the flowers, the moonlight, the strange sense of long standing familiarity with this unprecedented hour all help in some unthinkably precious way.

Being in the presence of a dying loved one draws us into this mysterious realm where, though nothing helps to spare the person from death, nor to spare us of their absence once they are gone, the smallest of things help in some ineffable way: You put water to the lips of the dying loved one, rearrange a pillow, simply sit with your hand on their shoulder, or you hold their hand. Nothing helps to reverse the dying process. And yet the sip of water, the physical contact, and the other equally sincere and heartfelt little things that one might do all help to awaken us to a boundless depth in which we, along with the one who is dying, are beyond the need for help . . . beyond need . . . beyond. . . .

Sometimes this nothing-helps-yet-the-smallest-of-things-helps awareness can come to us even after death has occurred. I experienced this when my grandmother died of cancer in my parents' home. The Sunday ritual at the time was for me to drop by my parents' home after Mass with my two daughters to visit. One Sunday, my mother answered the door crying, saying that grandma had just died. While my father and aunt stayed downstairs, I followed my mother upstairs to my grandmother's room. My mother knelt on the floor, crying as she held her dead mother's hand. My older daughter Kelly, who was four years old at the time, knew her grandmother and had some sense of the momentous nature of the moment. My younger daughter Amy, whom I was holding in my arms, was still too little to even try to comprehend what was happening.

We all came downstairs to join my father and my aunt. Someone called the funeral home and shortly a man arrived in a hearse to get the body. He wheeled a gurney into the main hallway, where we all waited while he went alone upstairs and returned a few minutes later, carrying my grandmother's body wrapped in a dark blue blanket. As he carried her downstairs we all instinctively stood up and silently gathered around the gurney as he placed her body on it and proceeded to buckle the straps in preparation for her transport to the funeral home.

In this collective silence my father, who was standing next to me, slowly reached out and, with his hand shaking badly from his alcoholism, carefully removed a piece of lint from the dark blue blanket. I grew up trying to survive my father's violence, a violence fueled by alcohol and stemming from some undealt with demon inside of him that had him doing things no loving father or husband would think of doing to his wife and children. When my father delicately reached out with a trembling hand to remove that piece of lint from that blanket I said nothing. I did nothing. Numbed by the shock of it, I felt nothing. But in that instant a door opened somewhere inside of me leading down a long hallway lined with memories of a little boy caught in the explosive rage of violent moments in which no tenderness could be found.

He reached out to take the lint off the blanket! It did not help to bring my grandmother back. It did not help to undo a past almost too tragic to think about. But, without helping, my father reaching out to remove that small piece of lint helped in some immeasurable way. There are some moments that ravage God's heart with beauty as they ravage us with the beauty of God, revealing us to ourselves as tender in our violence, as caring in all our orchestrations of not caring.

Michelangelo's famous statue the Pietà stands in our collective psyche as manifesting the help that shines through the moments in which nothing helps. Mary holding the dead Jesus does not help to bring him back nor to undo the cruelty and injustice that was done. But there in the flowing serenity of the timeless marble is a holding that embodies a presence that flows on and on, not helping us out of our plight, but rather awakening us to our plight as opening out onto vistas we cannot as yet understand.

As seekers of the contemplative way we can discern we are on the path which enhances to the extent we recognize that though nothing helps, the smallest of things helps in some inestimable way. Reading this book will not help. Nor will going on more retreats, or continuing to engage in any of our other spiritual endeavors in the fundamental sense in which none of these things helps to stay the course of our own death which is already in the mail, accompanied perhaps by a great deal of suffering and loss. Nothing helps to overcome our essential powerlessness to sustain ourselves in existence or to make certain that our best efforts will gain victory over how a particular unjust situation is hopefully going to turn out.

And yet, though nothing helps, the smallest of things help. The sun came up this morning and will surely set tonight. While out walking we stop for just a moment to talk to a neighbor we have not seen for quite some time. Or we sit in meditation, mindful of our breathing. None of these things help to rescue us from the inevitability of an already underway demise of who we think and imagine ourselves to be. But even so, we can discern in these seemingly incidental things that do not help a quiet holding that embodies and opens out onto vistas we cannot as yet understand, vistas in which we are beyond the need for help . . . beyond need . . . beyond. . . .

A third characteristic of those who have come to serenity in the face of death is that they reveal to us that the smallest of things manifest perfectly the mystery that we seek. Several years ago I received a phone call from a man who identified himself as a student that I had taught in a senior religion class in Cleveland, Ohio. In giving me his name he asked if I remembered who he was. I had to admit to him that I did not. He reminded me of how each year I would take a group of students on retreat to the Trappist monastery of the Abbey of Gethsemani in Kentucky. He asked if I remembered one particular incident in which a student got up in the middle of the night to sneak back into the monastery kitchen to get cookies. One of the monks caught the student in the act, told the abbot who then told me that if any similar incidents should occur in the future I would no longer be allowed to bring students to the monastery. I said that I remembered that incident very well. At which point the man on the phone said. "Well, I'm that student!" Immediately remembering who he was, I said, "Pat! How are you?"

He said that, unfortunately, he was not doing very well. He shared his story of how after graduating from high school and college, he went on to law school and became a successful attorney. He married an attorney. A few days after his wife found out she was pregnant with their first child, he was diagnosed with a malignant melanoma. He said he was now quite ill and asked if I would fly out to Cleveland to see him. I said I would.

When I arrived at his home I met his parents, his siblings, and his wife. I held his baby daughter. Then his father took me up to the master bedroom where a hospital bed had been set up. When Pat saw me he recognized me, but found it difficult to speak. He told me so, as if to apologize. I held his hand and said he did not have to say anything. "We can just be together," I said. "That's what really matters anyway." At which point he looked at me with that look of authority that dying people have and said, "that is what matters anyway." And so we sat together. Every so often one of us sharing this or that. But mostly we were in silence, with my hand on his shoulder. I recall feeling grateful for his honesty in sharing with me that he was having difficulty in speaking. And I recall, too, that I was keenly aware that I lacked the corresponding humility to let him know that I was having a hard time speaking too, due to being worried that having come all that way I would let him down by not knowing what to say.

Then, suddenly, he started to make efforts to sit up, saying that he wanted to touch his feet to the floor. I went downstairs and got his father, who coached me in helping him with a process that he had obviously performed countless times. His father put down the sides on the bed, and went to one side of the bed as I went to the other. We sat him up. His father eased his legs over the side of the bed and then we both scooted him toward the edge of the bed until his feet touched the floor.

There we were, the three of us—Pat's father standing on one side, I on the other, Pat sitting in the middle— no one saying anything. And then I could feel it filling the room—the vast, virginal nature of touching our feet to the floor! As this vastness rose up, encompassing the three of us, I became aware of Pat's father, wondering who or what was holding up this man who was having to hold his dying son. I thought of Pat's mother downstairs, his siblings, his wife and baby, and how incredibly sad the whole situation was. I was aware of myself in my insecurities of not knowing just what to do or say in the face of such overwhelming loss. But over and above all this I was aware of Pat, a man that I once taught in high school, who was now teaching me the incomprehensible stature of such a simple, fundamental thing as touching my feet to the floor.

We who are seekers of the contemplative way can discern we are on the path which enhances when we discern within ourselves this sense of reverential awe for such simple things as touching our feet to the floor. This awe, though at times charged with strong emotions, is never fundamentally simply emotional. To wake up in the morning, aware that we are about to swing our legs out of bed and touch our feet to the floor, is not to lie there hyperventilating with excitement that we are about to be mystically transported by the divinity of touching our feet to the floor. This awe is the quiet awe of the awakened heart's assurance concerning the inherently unbounded nature of touching our feet to the floor, of standing up and sitting down, of writing or reading this sentence on this page of this book in this moment.

A fourth characteristic of those who come to serenity in death is an ever deepening acceptance of their seemingly unacceptable situation. Their serenity seems to be, in fact, the flowering of an acceptance of themselves just the way they are, one with the way the present moment simply is.

Those who are dying help us to see just how difficult coming to serenity through acceptance tends to be. As part of my doctoral training I worked with a woman in a nursing home who was in her nineties. She was losing her eyesight and her hearing. She had advanced rheumatoid arthritis, which caused her chronic pain and physical disabilities. She was experiencing cognitive deficits, so that if she walked out of her room and down the hallway, she would become disoriented and need help finding her way back. On the small bulletin board over her bed were thumb tacked color photographs of her home, her flower garden and her little dog. She would tell me that more than anything else in the world she wanted to go back to her own home and she could not go.

Each time I visited her it would be clear to me that her suffering was quite distinct from her pain. Her pain was caused by her medical symptoms associated with her advanced age. Her suffering was the direct expression of trying to hold onto a life that was slipping through her fingers. Her cognitive deficits seemed to cause her the most distress because she was intact enough to see how her own mind, with which she was attempting to hold on to her life, was itself slipping away. Sitting with her I would see a mirror of myself and of all of us in that our suffering is distinct from our pain. Our pain occurs as the natural consequence of painful conditions and circumstances. Our suffering arises from inordinate desire, in which we predicate our sense of inner peace and well being on the extent to which we can make our situation to be the way we want it to be. Our self-imposed suffering dissipates to the extent that we accept reality as it really is.

The now well known work of Elisabeth Kubler-Ross designates the stages of denial, anger, bargaining and depression through which those who are dying tend to pass in the self-transforming process of coming to seren- ity through acceptance. The passage through these stages tends not to be neat and sequential. Some, in fact, get stuck at and die at a certain stage of the process without ever coming to acceptance. And those who do pass through the various stages tend to do so in a messy and circuitous manner in which each phase tends to be interspersed with moments of experiencing the phases that precede and follow it. For example, in passing through the phase of being predominately angry about what is happening, one might experience moments of gradually learning to accept one's anger, interspersed with moments of being overwhelmed with all that is occurring. And moments of being overwhelmed might send one back, for a time, to a barely-held-together denial of the too-much-to-bear reality of all that is happening.

As those who are dying vacillate between their dif- ferent moods and responses proper to each stage of the dying process, they are able to move on by way of real- izing that their suffering is only intensified to the extent they refuse to acknowledge and accept what is happen- ing to them. And inversely, they discover their burden of self-imposed suffering is alleviated to the extent they are able to maintain a balance between doing for themselves all they are still able to do as they simultaneously accept the ongoing intensification of their symptoms and the increasing diminishment of their powers. They move forward, with as little self-imposed suffering as possible, by choosing, as best they can, to accept being neither more nor less incapacitated than they, at any given moment, really are.[3]

What the dying tend to discover is that their desire to accept their moment by moment situation the way it really is tends to overshoot its mark. That is, they find themselves desiring to accept their situation more than they are actually able to do so. For all their good intentions, they are still subject to moments of rage mixed with despair. They see how human they are in being powerless to go through the dying process with as much grace and dignity as they desire to achieve. This failure to actualize their desire to reduce their suffering by accepting their situation causes them more suffering. What they come to discover, in a trial and error manner, is that their powerlessness to accept their situation to the degree they desire to do so is, in fact, part of their situation, which must itself be accepted.

What then tends to happen, however, is that this deeper, more expansive desire to accept themselves as they really are also overshoots its mark. In their ongoing moments of impatience, discouragement and all the rest of it, they painfully realize that they are powerless to accept their powerlessness to the degree they desire to do so. In the face of this unfulfilled desire to accept themselves as they really are they experience more interior and subtle levels of suffering, which, in turn, dissipate only in more interior and subtle levels of accepting themselves as they really are.

In this transformative process the dying embody and give witness to the truth of Gabriel Marcel's words, "We do not see the light. We are the aperture through which the light breaks."[4] At first glance it would seem that we could counter Marcel's assertion in pointing out that we do see the light shining through the aperture of the dying loved one's ever more childlike and enigmatic presence. This seeing of the light is our visceral awareness that, in being in the presence of the dying one, we are in the presence of what all life is about.

But if we look more closely at what is happening to us as we learn to be with a dying loved one, the truth of Marcel's words become more readily apparent. For we cannot authentically be with the dying and maintain a purely dualistic stance as an observer of the light that is shining through the aperture of the dying person's childlike serenity. We can authentically be with a dying loved one only in our willingness to become transparent ourselves to the light shining through us in learning to accept and share in what is happening to the dying loved one each step of the way.

The acceptance that brings serenity to the dying begins to encircle us as well as we come to realize that our own self-imposed suffering can be diminished only to the extent we choose to accept the situation as it really is. In a self-transforming process, continuous with that of the dying loved one, we experience our limitations in carrying out this choice when we discover we are unable to accept the situation as much as we desire to do so. Seeing this, we suffer, until this powerlessness is itself accepted as the way we simply are, poised at the cutting edge of our inability to be with the one who is dying in the way we desire. Then, as if breathing the air of a highly contagious condition of accepting a seemingly unacceptable situation, we ask: "Can I get you anything? Do you want another blanket?" In the sincerity and concern such questions express, we and our dying loved one are rendered mutually transparent to the light.

The entire process often entails periods of being painfully out of step with one another. The dying loved one may, at times, be miles ahead of us in accepting what we are not as yet even ready to acknowledge. At other times we may come to a level of acceptance that we can only hope and wait for the dying loved one to come to as well. A sense of contemplative community arises in the compassion inherent in waiting for, and catching up with, levels of acceptance one or the other has yet to realize. A sense of contemplative community is fulfilled in being one with the dying in moments in which the serenity that pervades their being pervades our being as well.

At first, and for quite some time, the self-transforming journey of coming to serenity through acceptance is a matter of the will. The dying one and all concerned move forward together in an ever deepening and more expansive acceptance of themselves as they really are in their oneness with the way the present moment really is. Toward the end, however, even the dying person's capacity to choose is itself lost. The fuel of selfhood finally spent, the flame of intentionality gone out, nothing is left but a bare nub of a breathing presence that will itself soon cease to be breathing.

When our loved one finally dies we are left to continue on. But we do so knowing our heart has been tutored, in a most intimate fashion, concerning what it means to move on in the only way that makes any real sense. This way of moving on is paradoxical with respect to the mind in that it consists of learning to understand that we cannot, and do not need to, understand what is becoming of us as we journey, day by day, into an ever more simple and expansive awareness of what simply is. This way of moving on is paradoxical with respect to the will in that the journey remains to some degree a matter of the will. The journey entails a perpetual willingness to reverence what is most real and precious in ourselves, others, and the earth that sustains us all. But the journey entails as well a perpetual willingness to see and accept our will as a flickering flame, completely flooded by, yet tenderly shielded by an all enveloping gentle light utterly transcending what the will can attain. This way of moving on is paradoxical with respect to the serenity that arises in seeing and accepting that our own life is moving day by day toward its own unthinkable end. While our ego trembles in the face of our own mortality, an underlying acceptance clears the mind and opens the heart. With the unquestioning clarity of a child we come to know and trust that when the moment of our death finally comes, we will be nothing other than the way we always are, one with the way the one unfolding present moment always is—forever vast, ungraspable, simply given, and divine.

We seek to live a more contemplative way of life so that we will not have to wait until we are dying to learn how to live. The contemplative path teaches us how to live by laying bare how powerless we are to be the contemplative person we deep down really are called to be. Seeing that our desire to live contemplatively keeps overshooting its mark, we suffer. The suffering continues until we learn to accept our powerlessness to be as mindful, as compassionate, as we desire to be. Then we see how, at a deeper, more subtle level, the desire to accept ourselves as we really are overshoots its mark. This causes yet more suffering until we learn to accept that we are powerless to accept our powerlessness to the degree we desire to do so. And so we follow a self-transforming path of an ever deeper, more expansive acceptance of ever deeper, more expansive levels of our powerlessness to be anything other than the way we simply are, one with the way the present moment simply is.

In meditation practice we experience directly how suffering is inexorably woven into life for the simple reason that desire inexorably overshoots its mark. We sit in meditation given over to the desire to be present, open, and awake, neither clinging to nor rejecting anything, only to discover that we are unable to be as present, open, and awake as we desire to be. Seeing this is so, we desire to be compassionate toward ourselves in our powerlessness only to discover that we are powerless to be as compassionate toward ourselves as we desire to be. And so it is with each aspect of meditation practice. Each embodies a direct encounter with ourselves as we really are, which when seen and accepted, embodies an encounter with our powerlessness to accept ourselves as we really are. As our sitting practice carries us into ever deeper, more expansive levels of acceptance, the opacity of the ego gradually disperses, giving way to an intimate awareness of ourselves as being the aperture through which the divine light eternally shines.

As our meditation and other contemplative practices helps us to habituate this stance of an ever deepening acceptance, we begin to see how we are being invited to practice acceptance in the most common place experiences of day by day living: You drop by the grocery store to pick up a few last minute items on your way home. There is only one very slow moving clerk checking out a long line of people, each with a cart loaded with groceries. As you get at the end of the long line, you are frustrated by what is obviously going to be a long wait. The self-transforming power of learning to come to serenity through acceptance is all right here. The line is neither longer nor shorter than it simply is. It is going to take neither more nor less time for you to check out your items than it is going to take. You are feeling neither more nor less tired and stressed than you are feeling. As effected by your present level of fatigue and stress, your efforts to avoid having an all out hissy-fit over the situation are going to be no more or less effective than they are going to be. In the deep acceptance of the whole situation that compassionately embraces whatever lack of acceptance of the situation may be present, an underlying sense of serenity can begin to permeate the moment. In ways as simple and unassuming as this, we learn to recognize and treasure the celestial nature of the commonplace events of daily living. In an ever more habitual stance of serenity born of acceptance, we are awakened to our oneness with God manifested in and as the way the one unending present moment is ineffably unfolding with an unhurried, and incomprehensible certainty not of our own making.

As a fifth and final consideration we can explore how those who have come to serenity in death graciously reveal to us the unrelenting nature of grace. I was once seeing a woman in therapy, whom I will call Susan,[5] who came to me seeking help with symptoms of low-grade, chronic depression. Susan lived alone, was successful in her profession, had no current external losses to deal with, but nonetheless, suffered from a subtle and pervasive feeling that her life was essentially meaningless and without purpose. As she would put it, "I start my day wondering whether it's even worth getting out of bed to go through the essentially meaningless ritual of another day."

In sharing her psychological history she reported that when she was growing up, her parents routinely violated her boundaries and the boundaries of her siblings who, following the example set by the parents, violated the boundaries of one another. Hitting, yelling, being told bathroom and bedroom doors could not be locked, then opening bathroom and bedroom doors without knocking, and reading family members' private letters and diaries were all part of an overall family pattern. In her adult years Susan had loaned a great deal of money to her siblings which was never repaid. Her siblings had also borrowed household items promising to return them, but then returned them broken or not at all. For these and other similar reasons, Susan had learned to establish a distance from her siblings which she regretted, but felt necessary to maintain in light of their repeatedly ignoring her requests to change their abusive behavior toward her.

Early in her therapy Susan received a letter from an older sister informing her that she had just recently been diagnosed with an aggressive form of cancer. The older sister went on to say that the reason for the letter was to ask if she could move in with Susan so that Susan could help her deal with her cancer. The letter presented a real dilemma for Susan. During the years when they were growing up together this older sister was one of the major sources of Susan's ongoing and fairly severe sibling abuse. What is more, Susan reported that in their adult years this older sister was one of the key players in the ongoing pattern of abusive behavior that finally resulted in her feeling that she had to distance herself from her family. It did not take Susan long, however, to conclude the only real choice was for her to tell her older sister that she could move in with her under the condition that she treat Susan in a respectful manner.

The sister agreed to the conditions, moved in, then promptly ignored the guidelines she and Susan had originally agreed to. Each week Susan would come into therapy distraught over her sister's latest behavior. On one occasion Susan came in particularly upset, saying that she came home to discover that while she was away at work her sister had a man come with a tractor to plow up her back yard. When she arrived at the house a truck was in the driveway delivering a large quantity of roses, bushes, and other greenery. When Susan expressed shock over what her sister had done, her sister became irate, saying, "How can you be so selfish and petty as to complain about your yard when I'm dying of cancer!"

As the weeks went by her sister's cancer rapidly worsened. Susan's therapy sessions were taken up with her efforts to cope with morphine pumps, sleepless nights, and other equally stressful aspects of the final stages of cancer. Then one session Susan came radiant. She said that just the night before something amazing had happened. In the middle of the night her sister's pain suddenly lifted, and she and her sister had a long talk, the first real talk they had ever had. Susan said, "In all her pain my sister has become childlike." She said, as she started to cry, "I found my sister."

In the weeks that followed Susan no longer felt depressed. Each week she would come into therapy sharing her latest conversation with her sister and processing the transforming effects her growing relationship with her sister was having on her. Then her sister died. Susan went through the grieving process and as she came out of her grieving her depression slowly returned. In the middle of one of her sessions, as she sat telling me about her meaningless, one-dimensional life I asked, "What became of the woman who used to sit with me so grateful and alive in sharing her moments with her sister?" Tears came to her eyes, followed by a long silence. And then she said, "I do not know what happened to her. She went away."

I said to her, "It seems that perhaps what has happened is that your sister, in her suffering and death, was taken to a very deep place, and in her love for you and your love for her, you went to that very deep place with her. In that very deep place you found not just your sister, but yourself." She said, still crying, "Yes. It is true. Just as I was beginning to come alive, my sister died and I died along with her. In losing my sister I lost myself."

Susan's sister had raised orchids. During her sister's illness Susan had developed a personal interest in orchid plants. In a bay window in her home was one particularly large orchid plant. As part of her therapy Susan agreed to tend that orchid plant and to sit before it every morning in silence as part of her daily meditation. One day she came in elated. "It bloomed!" she said. "The orchid plant bloomed." Then, in the same breath, she spontaneously added, even before she could try to grasp logically what she was saying, "It's me!" In that instant I was in the presence of a deeply alive woman risen from the dead. As we sat together processing what had happened, we were both startled by a clap of thunder outside the window (a rare occurrence in Southern California). We both spontaneously broke out laughing in the synchronicity of the thunder clap, evoking in each of us a simultaneous awakening to the unrelenting nature of grace.

The moment did not mark an end to her difficulties. Rather, the moment provided an internal reference point of contemplative experience from which she could learn to cultivate a more grounded openness to a bigger picture in which her loneliness and struggles could be experienced as playing their own part in the unrelenting flow of the graced nature of the life she was living. In the words of the poet Dylan Thomas, she found within herself, not an escape from her loneliness and struggles, but rather a direct experience of "the force that through the green fuse drives the flower." She tasted directly the sustaining presence of God, who through her sister's death, a blooming orchid, a thunder clap, a moment of shared laughter, revealed to her the depths in which she could never be truly alone.

We can discern we are on the path that enhances when we can discern within ourselves, not a secret power to solve our difficulties, but rather a childlike awareness of and faith in a depth of presence that invincibly sustains us in the midst of our difficulties. We can discern we are on the path that enhances when we find ourselves being at peace in our moments of musing what the future might bring. Then, looking deeper, discovering this peace to be expressive of our knowing and trusting that regardless of what the future brings, it will be, in its depths, the ongoing unfolding of what our life up to this moment has so miraculously been. For the future cannot but be the ongoing unfoldings of the unrelenting grace in which we are perpetually transformed and sustained, even unto, into, and beyond the unforeseeable moment of our own approaching death.

9. Discerning That Which Hinders

In the previous chapter we explored some signs by which to discern that we are on the path that enhances our contemplative self-transformation. In this chapter, we continue with the theme of discernment, this time focusing on the process of discerning and taking steps to correct the ways in which we hinder our contemplative self-transformation.

When contemplative experience awakens, and is followed in a sincere and committed manner, we are born again, enlightened, made wise in lofty matters of the divine. Such metaphors denote a transcendent awakening to a transcendent mystery actively surpassing all set limits. Then, in one continuous movement of self-transforming grace, the transcendence into which we are being lifted up occasions a descent of compassionate love down into the lowest and most fragile places within ourselves and all living beings. The higher we ascend, the greater the momentum of the descent. The greater the momentum of the descent, the more clearly the lofty nature of the lowest is revealed, the more clearly the transcendent nature of the fragile is realized. Discerning that which hinders our self-transformation entails discerning the ways in which we hinder ourselves with respect to both the transcendent and compassionate love dimensions of our self-transformation.

We can discern we are hindering ourselves with respect to the transcendent nature of our self-transformation when we see that our efforts in contemplative living are marked by attitudes of control and possessiveness, in which our egocentric self seeks to be the origin, means, and end of the fulfillment contemplative experience realizes. Examples of a possessive and controlling attitude with respect to origins of contemplative fulfillment include such things as imagining that our path of contemplative self-transformation has its origins in our efforts to be transformed. For example, we might find ourselves imagining that our decision to pray or meditate in a certain way, to read certain books, or to belong to a certain religion is bringing about, or is causing God to grant, the spiritual fulfillment we seek.

We can take steps to correct tendencies to imagine our contemplative self-transformation begins with our efforts to be transformed by remembering the essentially given nature of our moments of spontaneous contemplative experience. More specifically, we can recall those moments in which contemplative awareness unexpectedly dawns over the dark horizon of our ignorance as we are going about the tasks of a busy day. We might recall, for example, how it sometimes happens that while walking to the store or sweeping the floor, we are caught off guard by the spontaneous emergence of a subtle visceral tasting of the inherent holiness of walking to the store or of sweeping the floor. We can readily recognize that such moments of spontaneous contemplative awakening do not originate with our efforts to achieve or produce them by the very fact that they are granted to us prior to and beyond our efforts to achieve or produce them.

But is it not also true that contemplative experience arises no less transcendently in the midst of our meditation and other contemplative practices in which we anticipate and seek its arising? For as the self-transforming event of contemplative wakefulness begins to arise in the midst of our efforts to evoke its arising, the interior richness of the contemplative experience qualitatively transcends what our efforts alone could produce or account for. Thus springs the gratitude and humble awe that tends to accompany each renewed awakening of contemplative experience that arises in our meditation and in the midst of all that constitutes our daily efforts in contemplative living.

By calling to mind and renewing our faith in the transcendent nature of the origins of contemplative awakening, we are afforded a vantage point from which we can recognize and take steps to correct possessive and controlling attitudes concerning meditation and other practices in which we seek to awaken contemplative experience. If, for example, we catch ourselves sitting in meditation as if our practice were some kind of project by means of which we are attempting to produce or fabricate a contemplative awakening, we can gently remind ourselves of the transcendent nature of the arising of the contemplative experience we are seeking to realize. We can remind ourselves as we sit in meditation and engage in other contemplative practices that we are not attempting to produce contemplative experiences as the product of our efforts. Rather, we are seeking to heighten our vulnerability to the graced event of being ineffably awakened to our ineffable oneness with the ineffable.

We have been exploring ways in which we can learn to recognize and take steps to correct the ways in which we are hindered by possessive and controlling attitudes toward the transcendent origins of contemplative experience. We turn now to consider ways in which we can learn to recognize and take steps to correct the ways in which we are hindered by possessive and controlling attitudes regarding the transcendent fulfillment toward which our path of contemplative self-transformation is leading us. By this is meant learning to recognize and take steps to correct our imagined ability to see, from our present vantage point, just where our path of self-transformation is taking us, just where it is all headed. The issue here is not that we desire enlightenment, mystical union with God on this earth or eternal union with God in heaven, for it is only natural to have some understanding of and desire for the fulfillment of our heart's yearnings for spiritual fulfillment. Rather, the issue is that of a lack of humility in which we tend to forget that a journey that begins ineffably can only be fulfilled ineffably, which is to say, fulfilled unforeseeably, in ways that overflow anything we might think or imagine our fulfillment to be.

A good corrective measure for egocentric attitudes concerning the end or fulfillment of our path is to look back over our shoulder to reflect on the unforeseeable nature of the path up till now. Imagine, for example, that in cleaning out a rarely used closet, you come across an old journal that you had written, say, ten years ago. Sitting down you begin the read: The things you were into! The things you worried about! What you thought mattered! Where you thought things were headed! In some cases, it is true that the years bring such profound transformations that if the you that wrote that journal ten years ago could see the you that is reading it today, the you that wrote the journal ten years ago would faint! And yet we labor under the illusion we are finally figuring out what life is about. But to truly begin to figure out life is to accept its ultimately "un-figure-out-able" nature that leaves us delightfully perplexed, humbled, and grateful for a life we could not have planned if we tried.

Taking our contemplatively pondered past as our teacher, we can grow into a wiser, more contemplative understanding of the path that lies ahead and of the fulfillment toward which it is leading us. The pattern the past discloses suggests, that up to a point, we will be sustained in the predictable patterns of daily living. We all need some degree of daily predictability. We need to leave home in the morning knowing, with some degree of certainty, that our home will still be there when we return that evening. We need to know that we will be there at close of day to turn the key in the lock, to hear the familiar click, granting admittance, yet one more time, to an evening's rituals before getting into bed and going to sleep. And yet even a long life of sustained rituals of daily living brings its own unforeseeable changes. In the long arc of time the rituals of daily living turn like mill stones slowly grinding out a previously unexpected capacity to appreciate the boundless nature of the daily round of daily living. Whether we are considering the past in terms of year upon year of daily living, or in terms of the unforeseeable, precipitous events, in the aftermath of which we are never quite the same, the lesson the past has to offer concerning the future is the same. Unforeseeable events evoking unforeseeable transformations will no doubt continue to occur. The unrelenting passage of time will continue to transform us in unforeseeable ways.

Imagine, for example, an elderly couple sitting on a porch swing in the evening, looking back to when, years ago, as a young couple, they first built and moved into the house on the porch of which they now sit. Imagine them sitting there together, looking back to the children, now gone, looking back on the countless ups and downs, the gains and losses that form the story of how they have come to be who they thus far have come to be. Could they, as the young couple that sat for the first time on the porch on which they now sit have ever imagined, in any real or substantial way, the intimate qualitative texture of their present way of experiencing themselves and their life together? Hardly.

Humbly remembering the lessons our past provides us, we can better discern and take steps to correct any tendencies to presume that we, from our present point of view, can see the path that lies ahead. Humbled by memory, we can begin to understand and accept that our fulfillment on the path of self-transformation is unforeseeable. Instructed by the past, we will be able to understand that the goal toward which we are moving is not hidden from us in some kind of fog through which we are not allowed to see. Rather, it is hidden from us because the very way in which we presently see will be transcended as we continue to go through the ongoing metamorphosis that has so unforeseeably brought us to be who we thus far have come to be.

Our contemplative journey is one of being intimately awakened to the infinity of this self-metamorphosing process. Which is to say, our contemplative journey is such that we come to realize that our unfolding subjectivity is manifesting the unmanifested mystery we call God and the mystery we call God is manifested in and as our unfolding subjectivity. Saint Irenaeus said, "The glory of God is the human person fully alive." Living out, with all our heart, who we really are and are called to be is God's glory. It is "the dance of the Lord in emptiness." Up out of this emptiness arises the unending miracle of one's own simply given life, one with all the present moment simply is.

Humbled by a contemplative pondering of the self-transforming path we have traveled up till now, we come to see and accept that our present level of consciousness is simply incapable of grasping the ineffable fulfillment we seek. Given over to this humble awareness, our notions of ultimate fulfillment become transparent metaphors evoking a sense of mystery and hope. We speak of enlightenment, mystical union with God, the kingdom of God not as terms that we conceptually grasp, but as evocations calling us onward, toward an ever deeper awareness of an all encompassing, ever-present mystery that transcends all that we could possibly think or imagine.

Just as possessive and egocentric attitudes hinder us with respect to the origins and fulfillment of our journey, so too possessive attitudes hinder us with respect to the ongoing journey itself in which, if we are not careful, we can imagine ourselves to be the arbiter of our own ongoing self-transformation. That is, if we are not careful, we can catch ourselves imagining that we are at the center, orchestrating the process of learning to transcend our own egocentricity. When we are subject to this hindrance, we might find ourselves thinking and acting as if our progress on the path of self-transformation is essentially a matter of effectively carrying out our strategies and methods of self-transformation. Such self-referenced attitudes are ways of failing to realize that a journey that begins ineffably must move ineffably toward its ineffable fulfillment.

One sign by which we might discern that we are slipping into egocentric and possessive attitudes with respect to our efforts in self-transformation is that of comparing what we perceive to be our degree of progress with what we perceive to be progress made by others. If we perceive our progress to be less than we had hoped for, this comparative process might evoke feelings of jealousy or resentment over how advanced others seem to be compared to ourselves. Or we might find ourselves feeling discouraged or ashamed about how ineffective or inept our efforts in contemplative living seem to be compared to this or that person who seems to be so much more advanced than ourselves.

If, on the other hand, we are pleased with our progress, we might catch ourselves walking around with a certain air of mystical elitism and sophistication, in which our sense of self-esteem is embodied in a condescending attitude toward those we imagine to be not as advanced as we imagine ourselves to be. Or we might find ourselves resenting that others are not astute enough to recognize us to be the spiritual giant that we, in some interior, unacknowledged fashion, imagine ourselves to be. In the heady grandiosity of our own sense of spiritual attainment we might find ourselves offering unasked for guidance to others about how they should be or could be more contemplative. The smell and feel of egocentricity pervades such attitudes and imaginings, for in them all, one's wounded ego is at the center of the scene, trying to establish its control and basis for self-esteem in what it deems to be its degree of measured success in its efforts in transcending the confines of egocentricity.

One way in which we can correct the attitude that we are the final arbiters of own self-transformation is to renew and purify our commitment to our contemplative practices. Each practice calls us to lean, with all our might, into the pure flow of contemplative wakefulness, which, like water flowing from a rock, reveals the miraculous and simply given nature of the journey on which we find ourselves.

If, for example, your contemplative practice is writing poetry, the integrity of leaning directly into the void of waiting for a poem to appear reveals to you that you are not the arbiter of your life as a poet. You are surely responsible to sit and wait for the poem to emerge. You are responsible as well to hammer out, perhaps at a great price, the final nuances, the choice of this or that word. You remain, nonetheless, more the recipient of a gift than final arbiter of a project. You remain clearly one called to yield in transparent obedience to a graced stream of words flowing, not so much from you, but through you, to grace you and all who might care to listen. You remain as one who has come to learn from experience that each time you sit to write a poem you must do so with no reliance on a possessed track record of the poems that have been written thus far. You know that if you write poetry out of your accumulated storehouse of past poems, nothing new will emerge through the buzz of all the old poems that are trying to reappear, disguised as new, but easily recognized variations, old reworked songs already sung and spent.

In similar fashion, if your contemplative practice is fidelity to an intimate relationship, you come to learn from experience that each intimate encounter must be risked in its newness. In the ways of love, rehearsed lines and the mere rote repetition of mechanical acts ring hollow and leave the heart disappointed and unmet. So, too with prayer and meditation and with all contemplative practices—they remind us, by their very nature, that we are not the arbiters of our own unfolding self-transformation. In giving ourselves over to them we must let go of all self-referenced understandings of the path along which we are being transformed. We must lean, with complete abandon, into the perpetual newness of the mystery in which we are being perpetually transformed.

Through our renewed fidelity to our contemplative practices we learn to discern and take steps to correct any tendencies to drag around dust-gathering trophies of things past. The very simplicity that emerges in our whole hearted commitment to our contemplative practices frees us from boring ourselves and others with old war stories told over and over to prove to ourselves and others just how far we have come and all we have been through to get here. Sitting silent and still in meditation, walking with attentive gratitude at sunset, reaching out to cup the beloved's face in our hands, we find ourselves once again at the never ending origins of the one unending present moment in which our lives unfold.

We know by experience that in a relative, but very real sense, we are the arbiters of our journey, that we must take responsibility to cooperate with the grace of being faithful to our contemplative practices. If we do not meditate there will be no meditation in our lives. If we do not patiently work through the obstacles encountered along the way, we can lose our way and lose ourselves in the process. But at a deeper level, the entire journey is one in which we are called over and over again to surrender to a self-transforming process not of our own making. Each time we give ourselves over to our contemplative practices, what ever they might be, we find ourselves, once again, one with the communal mystery in which there is no separate self that is the final arbiter of the graced and endless ways of self-transformation into God.

It is true that as we pull back even the least little bit from our contemplatively realized oneness with the mystery we seek we cannot help but notice in our reflective awareness how the stream of gifted wakefulness is pooling ever deeper within ourselves. It's true that as we step back even further, we cannot help but see how we, in the midst of all our craziness and fragmentation, are being transformed into one who is learning to realize the ever more expansive nature of the way and the fulfillment it embodies. Rightfully received, this knowledge of ourselves as one on the way heightens our sense of humble gratitude for all that has been received thus far, accompanied by an openness to all that lies ahead. As soon, however, as we turn to possess, on our own terms, this path along which we are being dispossessed of our illusions of possessiveness, we become confused. We begin to lose our way, until, discovering how we have once again slipped into delusions of possessiveness, we humbly let go. And in this renewed stance of letting go, we realize ourselves to be once again caught in the updraft of grace in which there is no God, no no-God; no self, no no-self.

To speak of "no God" in this context refers to the fullness of a contemplative awakening in which God is no longer experienced as being dualistically other than the all encompassing totality that is realized. But this vanishing away of God as dualistically other than the all encompassing totality does not occasion the negation of God. To the contrary, it awakens us to the unmanifested mystery of God being manifested in and as all the one unending present moment really is. It brings us to the realization that ultimately only God is real, insofar as the word God denotes the endless origins, ground and fulfillment of "the all inclusive order of isness itself."[1]

Likewise, to speak of "no self" in this context refers to the fullness of a contemplative awakening in which we cease to experience ourselves as being dualistically other than the all encompassing totality that is realized. But this vanishing away of ourselves as dualistically other than the all encompassing totality does not occasion the negation of ourselves. To the contrary, it awakens us to the all encompassing totality manifesting itself in and as who we, in our deepest actuality, really are and are called to be.

Up till now the emphasis in this chapter has been on discerning and taking steps to correct the ways in which we hinder ourselves with respect to the transcendent nature of the origins, means, and end of our contemplative self-transformation. Our emphasis will now shift to discerning and taking steps to correct the ways in which we hinder ourselves with respect to the compassionate love dimension of our contemplative self-transformation.

It is worth noting that in real life the transcendent and compassionate love dimensions of the contemplative path are not laid out in sequential fashion, one after the other, but rather arise together as two aspects of a single unfolding movement of self-transformation. From the moment we are first awakened to the need to transcend our egocentric illusions concerning the origins, means, and end of our path of contemplative living, compassionate love is needed to help us face and accept how truly difficult the life-long process of dying to our illusions about ourselves really is. What we quickly discover is that the ascent into transcendence is not such that we instantaneously soar whole and complete, into an ever greater realization of our God-given oneness with God. Rather, the ascent is such that the illumined aspects of the self soar upward, even as other aspects of the self continue to be hurtful and insensitive, addictive and indifferent, and, in short, as intent as ever on remaining entrenched in fear-based possessiveness. Nor is it enough that we simply commit ourselves to overcoming these self-limiting tendencies. As we have just seen, our fear-based possessiveness finds its way into our very efforts to transcend it. Setting out on the path of self-transformation, we discover our egocentric self has decided to come along for the journey, trying each step of the way to be the origin, means, and end of the fulfillment contemplative experience realizes.

Let us then, by means of the following story, move on with our reflections, giving greater attention to the process of discerning and taking steps to correct the ways in which we hinder ourselves with respect to the compassionate love dimensions of our contemplative self-transformation: As I mentioned in Chapter 3, when I first entered the monastery I was assigned to work in the farrowing barn, where the sows gave birth to and nursed their litters. My responsibilities at the farrowing barn included going out into a large tract of fenced in wooded area to check the sows which ran loose with a large boar, which, as I recall, was named Nuclear Witness. When I found a sow that was getting close to having her litter, I was to tap and poke her with a cane, to get her to begin walking toward the gate that led out of the woods into a loading area where she would be taken to the farrowing barn.

The particular incident I wish to share happened on the first day I was being instructed by a senior monk on how to check the sow herd and lead a sow out of the woods. I recall following this monk out into the woods, as he headed straight to the area he knew the herd of sows would most likely be found. After finding the herd, he went from sow to sow. Without breaking the monastic rule of silence, he stopped at one sow, and explained with gestures and Trappist sign language that her teats were beginning to fill with milk. This was the main thing I was to look for in knowing when a sow needed to be brought into the farrowing barn to be scrubbed down with disinfectant soap and made ready to have her litter. Nodding to him that I understood, he began tapping and poking the pig with his cane saying, "Souey, souey." We were allowed to talk to the pigs, but not to each other. He prodded, poked and souey-soueyed the sow until she, with some protesting grunts, began moving in the direction of the gate that led out of the woods.

As the three of us, the experienced pig-monk, the pig, and myself walked along, I was suddenly handed the cane with gestures indicating that I was to continue tapping, poking and souey-soueying the pig. For me, a city boy, who had never even seen a pig up close before, this was quite a moment. Tapping her broad back, gently tapping her shoulders on the right, if she started veering off too far to the left, tapping her on the left if she started veering too far to the right, the three of us made our way through the woods.

All went well until we got to the gate, which was somewhat narrow. Since pigs are instinctively reluctant to go through narrow passage ways, the sow suddenly stopped at the gate, refusing to go through. There was a moment of indecision in which I, in my lack of experience, could think of only two options. I could try to force the sow through the gate by pushing and yelling and hitting her with the cane. But such violent tactics seemed unbecoming of a monk and besides the use of force with a three-hundred-pound brood sow seemed not to be the way to go. The other option was to leave the entire matter up to the sow, which would likely prove ineffective as well. If given the choice, the sow would most likely make a u-turn to go back to join her companions in their life of love and leisure in the woods.

Seeing the dilemma I and the pig were in, the senior monk took the cane. With a few whispered souey-soueys, and some seemingly effortless maneuvering, the three of us were suddenly going through the gate together! The passage through the narrow gate embodied the senior monk's compassionate attentiveness and response to the dilemma of the pig in her fear of going through the gate as well as my dilemma in how to get her through it. Compassionate love provided a third option, transcending the impasse created when I imagined that my choices were limited to either force or passive resignation.

A great deal of life can be likened to getting the pig through the gate. Getting the pig through the gate refers to the compassionate event in which an empathic attunement, a flowing through, a breaking open, a loving engagement transcends the limits of both force and passive resignation. In using this imagery I realize that some might find it in poor taste to lump ourselves in with pigs. But this concern arises out of a lack of appreciation for the noble pig, whose mysterious ways are, no less than that of a stallion or a bird on the wing, wholly permeated with the divinity all living things reveal. At any rate, we can now, by way of the pig-through-the-gate metaphor, focus on ways of discerning and taking steps to correct the ways we hinder ourselves with respect to the compassionate love dimension of our contemplative self-transformation.

I used to teach to high school religion. Teaching high school religion is getting the pig through the gate. High school students are, after all, not frequently inclined to engage in animated discussions on christology or morality. One option was to use force. Some teachers operate this way, using intimidation and threats to gain compliance and cooperation. But teachers and students alike are not fulfilled with this arrangement. It only writes another chapter in the sad story of those who have been traumatized in classrooms, and sadly, in some instances, in religious classrooms. Another equally ineffective option was for me to remain passive and allow the students to decide when and if they would ever decide to study their faith. Some teachers sometimes operate this way, passively babysitting a group of uncooperative students. But the teacher and students alike are not fulfilled with this arrangement either. It only writes another chapter in the sad story of a religion class in which no religion is taught. What I experienced over and over again is that compassionately being present in the room with the students cleared the way for us to go through the gate together. It held open the possibility that something relevant, fun, and lasting might happen for them and for me. Probably for must of us, if we look back to the teachers whom we most fondly remember and for whom we feel the deepest gratitude, we find ourselves remembering those teachers who not only knew but loved the subject matter. And, even more than this, genuinely loved and respected the students in a compassionate sensitivity to the challenges entailed in mastering the subject matter.

I am now a psychotherapist. A great deal of psychotherapy is getting the pig through the gate. Trying to force the client to see or do something he or she is not yet ready to see or do is never helpful. Being passive by failing to mirror back to the client the ways in which he or she is avoiding the root issues is never helpful. What is always helpful is a stance of compassionate empathy that creates a safe place in which the client can begin to feel what he or she really feels and to know what he or she really knows. The axial moments of therapy, that is, the moments on which the whole course of therapy quietly turns, often prove to be the moments of compassion in which the client and I pass through the gate together in a mutual experience of the graced presence that sustains and heals in the midst of the sometimes painful and destructive things that life brings.

Meditation is getting the pig through the gate. Intent on sitting silent and still we are, at times, agitated and filled with the noise of obsessing over what we think is the meaning of it all. At such times we are subject to resorting to force or to passive despair. But as we breathe compassion into the impasse, we are awakened, breath by breath, to the divinity of ourselves in our ineptness in present moment attentiveness. Breathing compassion into our powerlessness, our meditation embodies the Christ-event of God identified with us as precious in our powerlessness.

As we near the end of these reflections, let me emphasize one final time a theme that has been touched upon throughout these reflections; namely, the need to discern and take steps to correct the ways in which our contemplative self-transformation is hindered by our failures to compassionately love others. Ideally speaking, a commitment to contemplative living is synonymous with a heightened awareness of and response to the real suffering of real people. The difficulty however, is that our own wounded ego can circle about contemplative experiences in ways that make us less, not more sensitive to our own real needs and the needs of those around us. Religious faith, artistic inspiration, romantic-sexual love, the process of psychological healing, and all other arenas of contemplative experience and self-transformation, can and should be arenas of heightened compassionate sensitivity to the real needs of those around us. In our woundedness, however, these arenas sometimes become arenas of solipsistic living, in which we become less not more compassionately aware of and responsive to the sufferings of others.

The Jewish mystic and philosopher Martin Buber shares an incident in his own life which poignantly brings home the importance of discerning and taking steps to correct failures in compassionate love resulting in self-absorption with one's own religious experiences. Buber shares that one morning he was "filled with religious enthusiasm, a mystical ecstasy in which I felt myself in tune with eternity and the life beyond." Later that same day a young man came to Buber, saying that he was deeply troubled in struggling over the question of whether to choose life or death. Buber states that he was present to the young man, answered his questions, but due to an aura of the mystical experience that still hung about him, he answered only the questions put to him and "failed to see through to the man behind the questions." Shortly afterward the young man committed suicide. When Buber heard about the young man taking his own life, he experienced a kind of conversion, a metamorphosis of his understanding of what it means to be one with God. He writes:

> Since then, I have given up the "religious" which is nothing but the exception, extraction, exaltation, ecstasy; or it has given me up. I possess nothing but the everyday out of which I am never taken. . . . I know no fullness but each mortal hour's fullness of claim and responsibility. Though far from being equal to it, yet I know that in the claim I am claimed.[2]

Note that in the above passage it is not being lifted up into transcendence that Buber leaves behind, but a lifting up into transcendence that is understood as being nothing but a private exhalation set apart from life's concreteness. And note, too, that life's concreteness is experienced as having about it a quality of transcendence that Buber was humbly aware that he was far from being equal to.

The true artist is a contemplative, one who ponders and brings to light the hidden, precious nature of ourselves and the world around us. As such, the eye of the artist and the photographer, the soul of the poet, the ear of the musician should embody a compassionate, sensitive, and responsive stance to the pathos of human experience. But aesthetic experience, like religious experience, can easily take on mutated forms that leave one inspired in ways strangely oblivious and insensitive to the suffering of others. This was brought home to me during a trip my wife Maureen and I made to Santa Fe, New Mexico.

Santa Fe is known for its fine art galleries. In one gallery we saw a piece of contemporary art that was particularly striking. It was a table, the top of which was made from a large, old window frame that the artist had covered with beveled glass. A small placard on the table explained that the window frame was once part of a mental hospital that had been abandoned and torn down many years ago. The artist had made a table of the window frame by setting it on four elaborately carved wrought iron legs and then spraying the window frame and table legs with mint green paint specked with gold. Through the beveled glass top, I read the random scattering of cryptic graffiti that had been carved into the wood over a period of many years by the patients in the mental hospital: "Help," "Jesus," "I want out," "I want to die." These carvings made the table a piece set apart—something unique the artist came upon and set like precious stones in the work he had created.

I do not know the intention of the artist. He was, no doubt, aesthetically inspired and moved to create this piece. But the choice to paint this artifact of suffering a whimsical gold and mint green, the ornate legs, and the high price tag—all denoted an inspiration that remained hermetically sealed off from the suffering of those who had carved their cryptic messages into the wood. Whatever the intention of the artist may have been, however unfair or unwarranted my adverse reactions to the piece may have been, I must say that when I saw this table my mind immediately flashed to the men and women with whom I had worked in locked psychiatric facilities. I sensed, too, the presence of the men and women who had come to me for psychotherapy. In a moment of reverie I saw myself buying the table to give it a proper burial with candles and incense and chants of compassion for those whose souls still seemed, somehow, to linger in the crude carvings. Then I realized this ritual of compassion would have to embrace as well the artist who had made an artsy table from an artifact of human suffering. Then I realized the ritual of compassion would have to include all the times that I had so gotten into the diagnosis and assessment of a therapy client that I lost touch with the preciousness of the person and the felt reality of their suffering. I would have to extend the ritual of compassion to embrace us all in our collective propensity of becoming so caught in some insight or inspiration that we fail to see and go forth to identify with the suffering of all who suffer and are lost.

How many children are made homeless by poverty, severe parental abuse, war, or other conditions of extremity? How many men and women are homeless, hurting, and lost with no place to go? The security we all need in knowing the house we leave in the morning will be there when we return at night—how many do not, and perhaps never have and never will know this security? How many having external securities of all sorts, are bereft and lost inside in ways nobody sees? How often have we ourselves been the lost one that we ourselves would not acknowledge and take in? It is good for all who seek to live a more contemplative way of life to have questions such as these hovering about. Such questions authentically encountered, serve not as sources of despair or guilt, but as catalysts for an ongoing process of discerning and taking steps to correct ways in which our efforts in contemplative living can leave us less rather than more compassionately aware of and responsive to the real suffering of real people.

As a way of bringing these reflections to a close, I will share a dream that I had about five years after Merton's death. I was, at the time of the dream, writing *Merton's Palace of Nowhere,*[3] in which I explored Merton's notion of the true self one with God as distinct from the false self of egocentric consciousness. The dream helped me to discern and take steps to correct the ways in which I was getting so bound up with the project of writing a book about the true self that I was forgetting that the true self is expressed in an intimate, whole hearted engagement with the cosmic dance of my own life and the lives of those around me.

I dreamed that I was invited to attend a university to present a formal paper on Thomas Merton's principles of folk dancing. I believe this folk dancing theme came from Merton's interest in the Shakers. At any rate, in this dream I was in a large campus auditorium, filled with people who came to hear my presentation. The walls of the auditorium were wood-paneled and without windows. After I was formally introduced, I walked up on the stage, approached the podium and began, somewhat nervously, to read my paper, "Thomas Merton's Principles of Folk Dancing." As I got into the second page or so of my paper, all the lights went out, leaving the crowded auditorium completely dark, except for the small brass lamp attached to the podium which was illuminating my notes.

Somewhat startled by the lights going out, but without breaking my stride, I kept nervously reading on about Merton's principles of folk dancing. Then Merton appeared in the middle of the stage not too far from my podium! He was interiorly illumined, as a heavenly apparition should be, so I and all seated in the darkened auditorium could plainly see him, standing there, facing the audience, smiling, his arms folded across his chest.

I recall being surprised that he was there, wondering to myself, "What are you doing here? You're dead!" And I recall, too, feeling in the dream that I dare not look up from my notes because in my nervousness I might lose my place in front of all those people. I also recall resenting that Merton had showed up because he was ruining my paper on his principles of folk dancing! I could feel that everyone was so riveted on his presence that no one was paying attention to me as I continued to read my carefully prepared paper.

Then Merton, his eyes twinkling with laughter, began to do a folk dance! I, in turn, burrowed more deeply into my determined reading, as I felt all present were listening even less to all that I was saying. Then, out of the corner of my eye I could see someone out in the first few rows of the darkened room standing up and starting to folk dance with Merton. Then another stood and began to dance, then another, and another, until everyone in the room was folk dancing with Merton except for me, because I, with great frustration and determination, was reading on about his principles of folk dancing!

Contemplative wisdom discerns that we hinder ourselves in our ongoing self-transformation when we catch ourselves expounding, through clenched teeth, the principles of a dance that our own self-absorbed rigidity will not let us dance. But no matter how foolish and broken we may be, compassionate love is always ready to drain the fear-based rigidity out of the situation to the point that we might begin to recognize our ever present invitation to join in the general dance of God, one with us in our brokenness. The dance never ceases to stir within us, beating "in our very blood whether we want it to or not." The dance is deathless, childlike, and free; an infinite Presence wholly poured out in and as the concrete immediacy of who we simply are, beyond grasping in any way whatsoever.

Notes

Chapter 1
1. Thomas Merton, *New Seeds of Contemplation*, New York: New Directions, 1961, pp. 296-297.

Chapter 5
1. *The Gateless Barrier* is the title of famous collection of koans or Zen stories. An excellent translation and commentary of this seminal work has been written by the contemporary Zen master Robert Aitken. *The Gateless Barrier*, San Francisco: North Point Press, 1990.

2. The term "all encompassing totality" is inspired by Karl Jasper's work, *Reason and Existenz*, New York: Noonday Press, 1955. Jaspers, along with Gabriel Marcel, Martin Heidegger, and the classical philosophical traditions, give witness to philosophy as a contemplative path.

3. This phrase is taken from the thirteenth century Japanese Soto Zen master Eihei Dogen, who himself uses the phrase in quoting the Buddhist master Nagarjuna. See *Moon in a Dewdrop: Writings of Zen Master Dogen*, edited by Kazuaki Tanahashi, San Francisco: North Point Press, 1985, p. 31. A succinct and profound opening up of Dogen's teaching is found in Hakuun Yasutani, *Flowers Fall*, Boston: Shambala, 1996. I would be remiss if I did not acknowledge the extent to which my understanding of meditation has been nurtured by the work of the contemporary Soto Zen master Shunryu Suzuki, *Zen Mind, Beginner's Mind*, New York: Weatherhill, 1973.

4. Sermon 12 of the sermons of Meister Eckhart. Found in Bernard McGinn, F. Tobin, and E. Brogstadt (eds.), *Meister Eckhart: Teacher and Preacher*, Mahwah, NJ: Paulist Press, 1986. Thomas Merton observes that the Zen teacher D. T. Suzuki frequently quoted this statement of Eckhart as an exact expression of what Zen means by *Prajna*, that is, wisdom born of enlightenment. See Merton, *Zen and the Birds of Appetite*, New York: New Directions, 1968, p. 57.

5. Statement made in a conference at the Naropa Institute in Boulder, Colorado. A collection of some of the

conferences given by the Christian and Buddhist teachers at Naropa Institute can be found in *Speaking of Silence*, edited by Susan Walker, Mahwah, NJ: Paulist Press, 1987.

6. This statement of Eckhart was quoted by Thomas Merton in a conference given to the novices at the Abbey of Gethsemani. The conference is on cassette tape: "Thomas Merton: Life and God's Love," Electronic Paperbacks, tape 6 (but is now out of print). For a Buddhist rendering of the power of the breath to occasion and deepen the contemplative awareness of our oneness with the divinity of the present moment see: Thich Nhat Hanh, *Breathe, You Are Alive: Sutra on the Full Awareness of Breathing*, Berkeley, California: Parallax Press, 1988, 1990.

7. William Johnston (trans), *The Cloud of Unknowing*, New York: Image Books, 1973, pp. 48-49.

8. K. Kavanaugh and O. Rodriguez, *The Collected Works of Saint John of the Cross*, Washington D.C.: Institute of Carmelite Studies, 1991, pp. 189-190.

9. J. Blofeld (trans.), *The Zen Teachings of Huang Po*, New York: Grove Press, 1958, pp. 79-80.

10. *Moon in a Dewdrop*, p. 30.

11. Richard C. Clark (trans.), *Verses on the Faith Mind*, Fredonia, NY: White Pine Press, 1984, p. 1.

12. T. Cleary and J. C. Cleary (trans.), *The Blue Cliff Record*, Boston: Shambala, 1992.

13. *Moon in a Dewdrop*, p. 31.

14. This phrase is adapted from the title of a Buddhist work. D. Leighton, with Yi Wu (trans), *Cultivating the Empty Fields: The Silent Illuminations of Zen Master Hongzhi*, San Francisco: North Point Press, 1991.

15. See R. M. French (trans.), *The Way of a Pilgrim*, New York: The Seabury Press, 1972.

16. *The Cloud of Unknowing*, p. 56

17. This section was inspired by Sheldon Kopp's book *Back to One: A Practical Guide for Psychotherapists*, Palo Alto: Science and Behavior Books, 1977. In this book Kopp presents the psychotherapeutic process as one in which therapist and client learn together to "go back to one."

18. For a good introduction to Vipassana meditation for Christians see K. Culligan, M.J. Meadow, and D.

Chowning, *Purifying the Heart*, New York: Crossroad, 1994.
Also see J. Goldstein and J. Kornfield, *Seeking the Heart of Wisdom*, Boston: Shambala, 1987.

Chapter 6
1. The summary of boundaries presented in this chapter follows the approach presented by Pia Mellody. P. Mellody with A. Wells Miller and K. Miller, *Facing Codepencence: What It Is, Where It Comes From and How It Sabotages Your Life*, San Francisco: Harper and Row, 1989.

2. The theme of passing beyond boundaries and limits as it appears in this section was inspired by Robert P. Orr in his work *The Meaning of Transcendence: A Heideggerian Reflection*, Atlanta: Scholars Press, 1981.

3. A phrase used in the Buddhist scriptures to denote transcendent reality prior to and beyond all conceptual designations, including those of origin and end.

4. The poetic imagery used here and, indeed, throughout these reflections has been inspired and nourished by T. S. Eliot's *Four Quartets*, New York: Harcourt Brace Jovanovich, 1943, 1971.

5. A term used by Leon Bloy, the friend and spiritual mentor of Jacques and Raissa Maritain.

6. Taisen Deshimaru, *Questions to a Zen Master*, New York: E.P. Dutton, 1985.

Chapter 7
1. This section has been influenced by the work of D. W. Winnicott and other contributors to object relations theory. In a manner consistent with this book as a whole, object relations theory has been integrated with the work of Ken Wilber, Michael Washburn and other transpersonal theorists.

Chapter 8

1. *The Gateless Barrier*, p. 231.

2. A. F. Price and Wong Mou-Lam (trans.), *The Diamond Sutra and the Sutra of Hui Neng*. Berkeley: Shambala Press, 1969, p. 61. Thich Nhat Hanh has translated and written a simple and profound commentary to this important Buddhist text. See Thich Nhat Hanh, *The Diamond That Cuts Through Illusion: Commentaries on the Prajnaparamita Diamond Sutra*. Berkeley: Parallax Press, 1992.

3. The phrasing and basic point of view expressed in this section is based on the Buddha's teaching of the middle way as explicated by A. J. Bahm in his book *Philosophy of the Buddha*, London: Rider and Company, 1958. This section is also intended to be faithful to the essential spirit of Meister Eckhart's path of releasement (*gelazenheit*), see R. Schurmann, *Meister Eckhart, Mystic and Philosopher*, Bloomington: Indiana University Press, 1972/1978.

4. See K. Gallagher, *The Philosophy of Gabriel Marcel*, New York: Fordham University Press, 1975, p. 10. Gallagher takes this quote from Marcel's *The Mystery of Being*, Chicago: Henry Regnery Company, 1960.

5. The client referred to in this vignette has given permission for me to use her case here. Identifying information has been withheld or changed to maintain her anonymity.

Chapter 9

1. This phrase is taken from C. F. Kelley, *Meister Eckhart on Divine Knowledge*, New Haven and London: Yale University Press, 1977.

2. A. Hodes, *Martin Buber: An Intimate Portrait*, New York: Viking Press, 1971, pp. 10-11.

3. J. Finley, *Merton's Palace of Nowhere*, Notre Dame, IN: Ave Maria Press, 1978.

JAMES FINLEY

As a former student at the Abbey of Gethsemani, James Finley sat at Thomas Merton's feet in the "classical sense," laying a foundation for personal growth through fidelity to his own truth and inner-being. Drawing from both Buddhist and Christian sources, Finley shares the ways in which contemplative awareness in daily living can be cultivated. A clinical psychologist in private practice and a popular retreat leader, Finley has written several books, including *Merton's Palace of Nowhere* and *The Awakening Call*. Finley lives with his wife, Maureen Fox, in Marina del Rey, CA.